Building Bridges Not Walls

An Engineer's Guide to Theology

— PETER BOLD —

Sacristy
Press

Sacristy Press
PO Box 612, Durham, DH1 9HT

www.sacristy.co.uk

First published in 2020 by Sacristy Press, Durham

Copyright © Peter Bold 2020
The moral rights of the author have been asserted.

All rights reserved, no part of this publication may be reproduced or transmitted in any form or by any means, electronic, mechanical photocopying, documentary, film or in any other format without prior written permission of the publisher.

Scripture quotations, unless otherwise stated, are from the New Revised Standard Version Bible: Anglicized Edition, copyright © 1989, 1995 National Council of the Churches of Christ in the United States of America. Used by permission. All rights reserved worldwide.

Every reasonable effort has been made to trace the copyright holders of material reproduced in this book, but if any have been inadvertently overlooked the publisher would be glad to hear from them.

Sacristy Limited, registered in England & Wales, number 7565667

British Library Cataloguing-in-Publication Data
A catalogue record for the book is available from the British Library

ISBN 978-1-78959-094-4

Contents

Why Write? 1

Part 1 11
1. How Our Understanding Grows, and Why We Get So Angry ... 13
2. How Do We Do Theology? 21

Part 2 29
3. Does God Exist? 31
4. How Reliable Are the Gospels? 43
5. What about the Old Testament? Treasure or Texts of Terror? 61
6. So Who Was Jesus? 77

Part 3 91
7. Why Did Jesus Die, and What Does That Say about God? 93
8. Why Did Jesus Come Part 1: The Kingdom of God 107
9. Why Did Jesus Come Part 2: The Holy Spirit 118
10. The Spirit Leading the Disciples into all Truth 132

Part 4 141
11. Who Goes to Heaven? 143
12. Sexuality and a Divided Church 156

Part 5 167
13. Faith without Works is Dead: Growing the Kingdom of God ... 169
14. Growing the Kingdom of God Part 2: Changing the World 180
15. Truth, Global Warming, Post Modernism and Politics 189
16. My Journey and Hope for the Church 196

Notes 199

CHAPTER 1

Why Write?

When I was twenty-eight years old, I stopped working as a research engineer, specializing in metal fatigue in railway lines, and started training at Durham University to become a Church-of-England vicar. The transition was quite a shock. This book tells some of my story: how I as an engineer have struggled with the world of faith and theology, and how for me an engineer's approach has proved helpful. I hesitated to call the book *An Engineer's Guide*, as I wasn't sure I was qualified to be a guide. I write as someone who has "been this way before" rather than as an expert.

I had thought of calling the book *An Engineer's Struggle with Theology*, but that would be too negative. I have found the struggle life-giving. By working through some of the academic debate, and questions concerning suffering, my faith is on firmer foundations. It has also kindled a passion for putting my conclusions into practice and sharing my journey. I believe that good theology is vital for the health and unity of the Church, and its mission in the world. It has been a fruitful journey, though I am left with unanswered questions.

My training as an engineer emphasized the need to communicate with those who are not experts. Part of the struggle I had with theology was that I found many academic books difficult to read, and unnecessarily long and complicated. As an engineer's guide I am aiming to communicate what I consider to be crucial theology in a concise, comprehensible form: my complete or systematic theology in 60,000 words.

As an engineer, there was no point doing research or designing a machine, if the work just stayed on a computer, or a drawing board. The whole point was to move forward the boundaries of knowledge, sell a product, or make money. In writing this book, my motivation is different, but I still want to make a difference. Hence the title, *Building Bridges Not Walls*. I don't want theology stuck in ivory towers. I don't want to build walls just to defend the Church or my faith and keep other ideas out. A bridge built on solid foundations enables interactions with those from different backgrounds, and hopefully through that we can all learn and make the world a better place.

I might have also called the book "a vicar's guide to theology", because like engineers, vicars are involved in the real world. At Durham, we studied theology in a rather academic setting, answering the questions the examiners set. Now, as a vicar, the issues and approaches are different. The book is not just about my time at university, but about my journey from childhood until now, the interaction between academic theology and the real world. A journey that has at times been a delight, and at times a struggle. A journey that is not complete.

How do we "do theology"?

The first section of this book concerns how we actually do theology. How can we know anything about God? How can we judge between conflicting answers? In engineering, we tackled problems and disagreements by going back to first principles: Isaac Newton's laws of motion, the laws of thermodynamics or the "scientific method". When I did my degree in engineering, I started with those foundations and built on them. In contrast, when I arrived at university to study theology, we leapt into questions and ideas about theology, without giving much time to the process. I felt rather at sea. We explored Old Testament theology, Pauline theology, Johannine theology, liberation and feminist theology. We considered, "What did St Paul think?" rather than, "Was St Paul right?" All ideas were considered to be good ideas.

The real world I inhabit as a vicar is very different. Some groups claim that one particular set of beliefs or practices is right and beyond dispute, while others claim infallibility for a contradictory set. There is no agreement as to whether God exists, let alone whether the Bible or the Qur'an gives a more accurate picture of him. Sadly, all too often our response to those who disagree with us is to avoid the subject, or to avoid the people. So evangelical Christians go to evangelical churches, Anglo-Catholics to Anglo-Catholic churches, Muslims go to mosques, and atheists avoid church altogether. Tragically at times disputes have led to violence, verbal or physical, rather than listening.

And yet, as an engineer, I wanted to know why people thought different things. If one engineer thought something would break while another thought it was safe it would be criminal not to find out why they disagreed. Key to understanding disagreements was to ask how others came to their conclusions. How do they do their theology? To ask them to tell their stories. I want to build bridges, not walls.

Do the answers matter?

In engineering, getting the right answer matters. At the beginning of my research in metal fatigue, I designed some new grips and specimens to try to recreate the stresses in a rail when a train passed over it. Most of my research budget was spent making these specimens and the grips before I could begin my testing. If my design was not right, the grips could have broken instead of the specimens, and all the money would have been wasted. After producing my first set of drawings, I showed them to a technician, who immediately spotted a problem. I was glad I asked and followed his advice. He was right. In engineering outside of universities, people's lives as well as their money can depend on getting the answers right.

In theology, many people think that getting the right answer doesn't matter. Faith is considered a private affair and to discuss it likely to cause offence. And it can cause offence. But some of the issues of faith are far more significant than my engineering. My faith led me to change career. For millions of martyrs over the centuries their faith has led them to lose their lives, trusting that a better life awaited them. For most of us, our faith or lack of it has consequences for how we live our daily lives, spend our money and conduct our relationships. It is not a purely academic exercise. The answers matter enough to listen to others in case I am wrong.

Surely faith and science have nothing in common?

At school, most of us have performed experiments in science lessons, demonstrating perhaps that the current in an electrical circuit is equal to the voltage divided by the resistance, or that acceleration is proportional to force divided by mass. As a result, many people think that all "science" can be proved in laboratories, and that therefore questions of faith are unscientific.

However, science isn't all like that. The theories of evolution or the "Big Bang" cannot be proved in a laboratory. They result from observations of our world and universe as it is now, including fossils and the movements of galaxies. The theories of evolution and the Big Bang are logical deductions from those observations. I believe in both, but technically they are theories. They cannot be proved by recreating them in experiments, as we can with Newton's laws of motion. From my own field of engineering, when something breaks, you cannot find the cause of the fracture by putting it back together and testing it. But you can look at the pieces. The history of the object may be revealed in concentric markings on the fracture surface, growing out from a crack origin.

My approach to my faith is similar. We cannot reproduce the events of the Bible, but the fact that we have the Bible, and in particular the New Testament documents, and the fact that we have the Church today, means that we have somewhere to start. Their existence is an undisputed fact. My faith is in part my reasoned response to these facts.

Christopher Hitchens, in his arguments against the existence of God, states:

> What can be asserted without evidence can be dismissed without evidence.[1]

As an engineer, with a scientific background, I agree. However, unlike Hitchens, I believe there is evidence for my faith. It is like sitting by a pond and hearing a splash, looking up and seeing ripples moving out from a point on the surface. Something must have caused the noise and the ripples. However, from the noise and ripples alone you could not tell whether the splash was caused by a fish, or by a stone being thrown in the pool. Unless there is another splash, you can only use reason to narrow down the possibilities.

The result of my study and reasoning is that in some areas of faith I am confident to declare what I believe. I would not claim they are a proof beyond all doubt, but they have convinced me enough to radically change how I live my life. In other areas I am less certain.

Approximations and tolerance

In science, disagreements still occur. But, by going back to first principles, the reasons for them and the range of uncertainty can in theory be seen. In the current discussion as to the effects of greenhouse gases and the dangers of global warming there are differences in the predictions made by groups of scientists. However, these disagreements are not about the fundamental process. All agree that carbon dioxide is a greenhouse gas, and that carbon dioxide is produced by burning fossil fuels. The differences arise because the world and our weather systems are so complicated that it is impossible to create an exact model with an exact answer. No scientist would insist that their model was perfect. The common understanding of the science and the modelling process allow real discussion to take place as to the merits of the different models and the range of uncertainty. Among climate scientists, there is agreement about the heart of the process, and also agreement about the uncertainty of predictions.

Equally in engineering, it is impossible to make something to an exact size or weight. With the right technology and expense, the error may be minute, but the errors remain. In the world of engineering answers are generally given as approximations. Where size or weight is critical, specifications are given with tolerances: instead of 10mm, 9.99 to 10.01mm.

I cannot tell, but this I know

In my approach to theology, I think a similar tolerance is crucial.

When I was growing up in Birmingham, when people said, "I'm not bothered", it meant they didn't mind either way. Moving to South Yorkshire I discovered that for others, "I'm not bothered" means "I don't like". The same words can mean different things in different contexts and cultures.

The New Testament was written nearly 2,000 years ago, in Greek, and in a different culture. Jesus spoke Aramaic, not Greek. He often taught using parables, which are subject to interpretation. We cannot tell the tone of voice he used, or fully understand the cultural context in which he spoke. When we add to that the vastness of the Bible and its many and varied forms of literature, we should be cautious in declaring what we think it means.

I love the hymn, *I cannot tell . . . . But this I know*. There are some historical facts that I consider to be beyond all reasonable doubt. The heart of my faith is built on them. There are also significant issues that raise doubts for me, in particular the fact of so much suffering in the world. I believe in the death and resurrection of Jesus with a confidence that affects how I lead my life every day. But I cannot give a good answer as to why there is so much suffering, and so I respect those who disagree with me.

Modernism and Postmodernism

So I believe that by looking at evidence, going back to primary sources, we can know the truth, or we can estimate uncertainty. In philosophical terms I might be described as a modernist, relying on logic and the scientific method. At Durham we were told that our culture had become "postmodern". The horrors of war and environmental disasters, made possible by modern engineering, were said to be in part responsible for this cultural shift. Alister McGrath in his Introduction to Christian Theology states that in our postmodern culture we have stopped having confidence in the power of reason to provide universally accepted foundations for knowledge, especially in the areas of faith and morality. Instead, relativism and pluralism—the belief that contrasting "truths" are equally valid—has flourished.[2]

In a lecture, postmodernism was described as having a pick n mix approach to truth—selecting what you like.

The strength of postmodernism is that it has encouraged people to think for themselves, rather than being dictated to by the Church or any other "custodian of truth". Scepticism, not trusting everything we hear, is a strength when it leads to proper investigation. But I worry that instead of investigating, many are simply choosing what to believe or not believe based on a personal preference.

In his novel *The Da Vinci Code*, Dan Brown alleges that Jesus was married and had children, but that after his death the Church hid these facts and distorted his teaching. The Church hierarchies were described as a male conspiracy hiding the truth. I enjoyed the book as a thriller, but was frustrated to hear of many people who thought that it might be true. I watched interviews on the BBC where two male clergy stated that it wasn't true—but if you believe that the Church is a misogynistic conspiracy, what else would they say? I didn't hear of the BBC going back to historical sources or any other evidence. People were believing what they wanted to believe. I found it frustrating. Then Graham Norton on his show mentioned the book and said "if you don't want to know what it is about look away now". He then held up a card which said it is all b******s. Many people stopped taking the book seriously after that.

I was grateful for Graham Norton's contribution, but worried that many people's beliefs were based on what celebrities say or popular culture, rather than looking at the evidence.

Making a difference in the world

As an engineer I am concerned for practical action, not just head knowledge. As the letter of James says, faith without deeds is dead (James 2:17). So, in the final chapters of the book, I will consider issues about how we put our faith into practice.

Engineering in the real world lives with uncertainties, but by building on solid foundations, it has achieved extraordinary feats. Engineering includes approximations, safety margins, and sometimes having the humility and honesty to say we don't know. But that humility has not stopped us putting people on the moon.

All Christians agree, at least in theory, that Jesus commanded us to love our neighbours, and that this includes our enemies. Sadly, we have often failed to put that command into practice. Yet where Christians have put aside their differences, and have united around what they agree on, they have made an amazing difference in our world.

Christians have played a significant role in abolishing legalized slavery, bringing peace in Northern Ireland, and developing charities and fair trade around the world. Indeed, it is extraordinary to think that Christianity has spread all over the world, despite the imperfect way that many have attempted to share their faith over the centuries.

Rather than uniting around all that we agree about, the Church has often fallen out over matters that are uncertain. We have spent our energies debating things of lesser importance, rather than looking at the crucial questions and working together with our common faith to make the world a better place.

The myth of objectivity?

As an engineer I was taught that in reports we should always write in the passive voice: "a force was applied" rather than "I applied a force". The theory behind writing in this passive voice was that the person doing the experiment should not be significant in the findings. However, when reading reports, we always considered who wrote them. In the world where big business and science interact the author is even more significant—are they representing a particular vested interest?

Equally in academic theology, the accepted style is to write as an impartial observer. But might the subject matter affect future book deals or academic promotion?

So, this is my story. I am a Christian who gave up an engineering career to be a vicar, and my financial future rests on the Church of England. More significant than financial concerns for me, however, is that many of the issues discussed in this book are intensely personal, and it does feel frightening to "bare my soul". What will people think of me?

The dinner party advice of avoiding talking about politics and religion would be much safer!

In the light of this, before moving to how I think we should "do theology", I think it important to consider the tensions and anger that can surround matters of faith. In that sense, the ways we learn and practise theology are very different from the ways we learn and practise engineering.

PART 1

How?

CHAPTER 2

How Our Understanding Grows, and Why We Get So Angry

It might surprise you to know that we studied some psychology in my engineering degree. Engineering is fundamentally logical. It builds on the foundations of the maths and physics we learn at school. But when it comes to marketing, or working in teams, then it helps to know some basic psychology. For example, the Millennium Bridge crossing the Thames in London had to be closed for a while, because it wobbled too much. On the news at the time, the engineers who designed it insisted it was not dangerous, but the general public didn't feel safe. The bridge had to be retrofitted with dampers to stop the swaying.

Similarly, the first time I climbed an aluminium ladder to paint the gutters on my house, I felt unsafe because of the way my ladder bent under my weight. The ladder was not going to break. If I had done the calculations, I could have proved it. I know that aluminium can bend elastically and spring back without any problem. But when I first climbed the ladder I was scared. My engineering knowledge was not enough to quench my deep-seated fear of falling.

Engineers need to appreciate this basic psychology if they are going to successfully market anything that is new. To some extent we all make decisions based on feelings rather than logic.

In this book, I will explain the logical foundations for my faith. But my faith didn't grow that way. For most people faith develops through a mixture of intuition, experience and interactions with parent figures and peers. In theology, an understanding of basic psychology is key to understanding the emotions that so often surround issues of faith and religion.

Sometimes the violence done in the name of Christianity or other faiths is the violence of political power games, but that is not always the case. I have seen a number of Christians become furious with others because they hold different views. I've never seen anger of that sort in engineering. It occurred to me that anger of this nature derives from the personal way in which people often come to their understanding of spiritual issues.

The book *I'm OK—You're OK*[3] is an introduction to one theory of relationships, and of how we start learning from birth. I read this book following our introduction to psychology in my engineering degree. The logical, almost mechanical structure of its argument appealed to me as an engineer, and it made sense to me. This forms the background to what follows.

How we learn as children

Our initial learning as children may be represented like this:

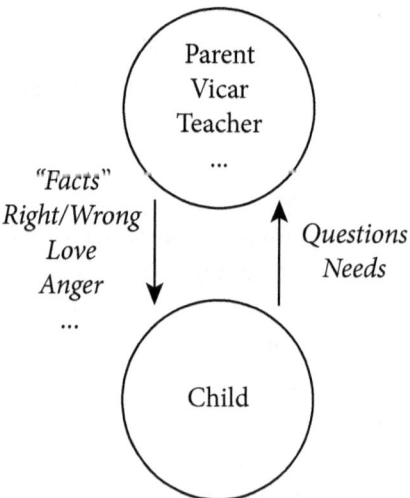

We learn from our parents, or other parent figures. Most of us accept what we are taught without doubting the teacher. We may ask questions for clarification, but we do so assuming our parents or teachers know best. For most of us, the majority of the "facts" and guidance given by our parents will have been helpful and uncontroversial. As children we cannot work out everything for ourselves from first principles. Much of our formal and informal education with new teachers and parent figures will build constructively on those early experiences. As we grow older, we will pass down those same lessons and values. This form of learning is hierarchical—the child may ask questions, but the parent figure provides the answers.

This then can lead to a "domino effect":

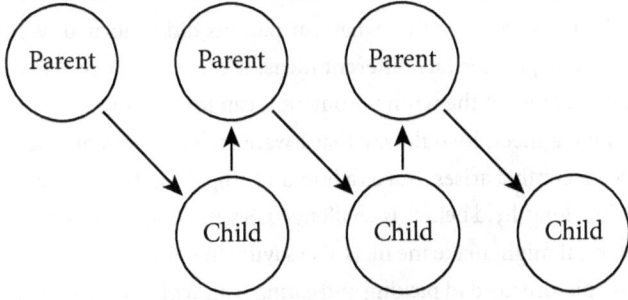

Most children, in time, become parent figures who teach their "children" the facts and values they were taught. In this way knowledge and conventions are passed down from one generation to the next.

Causes of conflict

However, problems and conflict can then arise when we encounter people with different views.

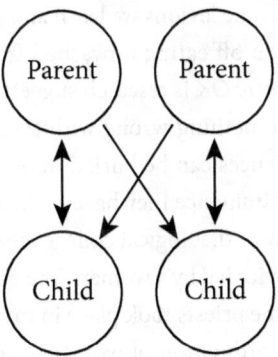

For example, when I grew up, we regularly ate fruit straight from the trees and bushes in our garden. It never did me any harm. Others I have known wouldn't dream of eating fruit from a garden without washing it first—"it will be covered in germs . . . ". I'm not a microbiologist, so I don't know what the real risks are from a garden strawberry.

As a vicar, when I am involved in marriage preparation, I have asked couples to share with each other how they would expect to divide household chores, handle their finances or spend their leisure time. On many issues we assume that what our parents did is normal. When we discover our partner has different ideas, it can be a shock. When that discovery comes at the wrong moment it can lead to rows.

As an engineer, I would say that I want to have rational discussions whenever conflict arises. But as a human being, I can feel deep distress if one of my long-held beliefs is challenged. Saying that the strawberry I'm about to eat might make me ill, is also saying that my father was wrong. I can still picture my dad picking and eating fruit without washing it, and I love and respect him. Saying he is wrong is a much more emotional issue than the microbiology of a strawberry. I don't have that sort of emotional attachment to those who taught me engineering.

When it comes to questions of faith, including atheism, we often learn our beliefs and traditions from people we love and respect, or from a time in our lives when we felt most secure and loved. Encountering others who disagree with us disturbs those memories, and so may provoke reactions out of proportion to the surface issues involved. The issues are also much more personal than the issues of engineering.

We all have negative experiences as well. These uncomfortable memories can also become lessons we learn and pass on. One bad upset stomach might put you off eating unwashed fruit for life. Behind the book title *I'm OK—You're OK* is research suggesting that many grow up feeling that there is something wrong with them—they are "not OK". These negative experiences can be buried in our subconscious, so that we are unaware of the influence they have on how we think.

I remember the day at theological college when for the first time we had a communion service led by a woman. The vote in General Synod to allow women to become priests took place in my first year. I had always been in favour of the ordination of women—values taught me by my parents and others who nurtured me in my faith. Logically, I had worked through the arguments. However, in that first communion service, led by one of our lecturers called Alison, I started with an odd, uncomfortable feeling.

I had been to a boys' secondary school with no women teachers when I started, and then I had studied engineering with no female lecturers. The only significant female authority figures I had encountered since primary school were my mother and Margaret Thatcher. I did not have a perfect relationship with my mother and had not liked Margaret Thatcher (or the media's portrayal of her). I think my uncomfortable feeling was caused because I did not want either my mother or Margaret Thatcher as my vicar.

Within minutes of the service starting the discomfort disappeared, because I was delighted with the way Alison led the service. I was already impressed with her leadership, passion and pastoral care. The memory serves as a reminder to me that my emotional reactions are not always governed by the logic in my head, and the logic in my head might be distorted by memories hidden in my subconscious.

Healing through listening

I also remember going to a conference in Northern Ireland about twenty years ago. The peace process was moving forward, but there was a long way to go. On the first day we went to the ITV studios in Belfast, and they showed us a series of news clips, depicting the history of the troubles. As I watched, I realized that my picture of recent Northern Irish history was distorted. I was well aware of the violence of the IRA. I had lived in Birmingham at the time of IRA bomb threats. Going to bed one night our house was shaken by a bomb exploding underneath the car of Labour MP Dennis Howell, who lived on our road. I knew also of the IRA bombs that had killed Lord Mountbatten, and that had killed and injured so many at the Conservative party conference in Brighton. In the ITV studios that day I realized that I knew nothing of the violence of the Unionists.[4] My picture was one-sided. That side might be true, but it was not the whole truth. Having seen the news clips, the so-called peace walls dividing the city, and the murals glorifying the violence, we went to bed depressed.

The next day we went on a coach trip up the spectacular coast road heading north. We arrived at the Corrymeela Community. They told us how they brought together teenagers from the two sides of the conflict. They would start with games and relaxation in the wild and peaceful countryside. Then in the evenings they gathered the teenagers together and encouraged them to share their stories, their individual experiences of the troubles. Both sides could then begin to see more of the whole picture. And wonderfully, I would say miraculously, healing began.

I hope that the transformation that has come in Northern Ireland will inspire everyone to listen to those we disagree with. The healing in places like Northern Ireland is extraordinary. Sadly, the rows I have witnessed over the right way of worshipping are also extraordinary for the opposite reasons.

I learnt from the Corrymeela Community that a healthy approach to theology involves listening to those we disagree with. This enables us to understand why others believe and behave the way they do. In terms from *I'm OK—You're OK*, we engage our "adult", instead of just behaving as a parent or a child:

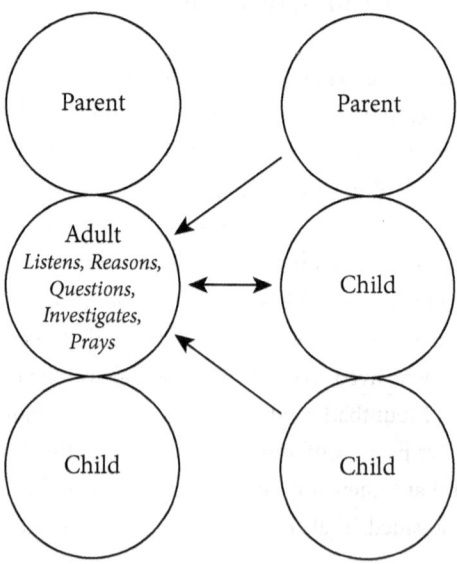

Our "adult" has the humility to accept that none of us know the whole truth. The Gospels are full of stories of how the disciples got things wrong. Our adult recognizes that even those who have loved us and taught us are not perfect. So we listen and ask questions so that we can understand more of the whole picture.

As I said in the first chapter, the answers matter enough to listen to others in case I am wrong.

Right beliefs and right relationships

But I am not just concerned with getting correct answers. Consider two words I learnt at theological college, and a discussion I had with my local Baptist and Methodist colleagues when I gave talks on some of this material:

- **Orthodoxy** is concerned with correct belief. If you are orthodox you "believe the right things". "Ortho" comes from the Greek for straight or true, and "doxy" from the Greek for belief.
- In South America, with the development of liberation theology, a new word was emphasized: **Orthopraxy**. Praxis is Greek for action. Liberation theology emphasized that our actions are more important than our beliefs. Jesus said the most important commands were to love God and to love our neighbours. That love involves action, not just belief.

In the discussion with my colleagues we spoke of the need for a new word for right relationships. In our churches we can be so concerned with believing the right things, or doing things correctly, that we can forget the people involved, and that some might have different ideas.

My Methodist colleague told us of a popular quote by John Wesley:

> In essentials, unity; in non-essentials, liberty; and in all things, charity.

Jesus said:

> You have heard that it was said, "You shall love your neighbour and hate your enemy". But I say to you, Love your enemies and pray for those who persecute you, so that you may be children of your Father in heaven . . . For if you love those who love you, what reward do you have? Do not even the tax-collectors do the same? And if you greet only your brothers and sisters, what more are you doing than others? Do not even the Gentiles do the same?
>
> Matthew 5:43–47

If we only love those who believe the same things as us, like to worship in the same way as us, or have the same musical tastes as us, how are we different from the members of a golf club?

In this book, I will tell some of my story, as I have tried to find right belief. I will go on to consider the actions I feel we should take in response to that belief. I pray that through it all, better relationships will grow, that we will come to understand those we disagree with and love them even if we cannot agree.

CHAPTER 3

How Do We Do Theology?

When using this material in a lecture, I have asked the audience to guess how much I weigh. Behind the guesses lay different sources of information. They could see how tall I am, and my build. They probably knew what they weighed. The audience could therefore use reason to combine their knowledge from different sources. No one has suggested I weigh less than ten stone or more than sixteen. The fact is I do not know exactly what I weigh. I do not know how accurate my bathroom scales are and my weight will change during the day. However, as I write, I can say with confidence that I weigh between thirteen and thirteen and a half stone. When I go rock climbing, I am happy to trust my life to a climbing rope designed to hold much greater stresses.

My approach to theology is similar. We do have sources of information. We can use our reason to combine them. They will not give us exact answers. There are many issues where there is uncertainty. However, in spite of that uncertainty, I am willing to trust my life to the heart of my belief.

Four sources for faith

One helpful lecture at Durham introduced me to four sources for studying theology:

- Scripture
- Tradition
- Experience
- Reason[5]

This gave me a framework for understanding different approaches to theology and matters of faith. We differ in the priority we give to one or more of these sources. Some emphasize the Bible as the source of all authority, whereas others put a greater emphasis on the tradition of the Church. Scientists and philosophers might prioritize reason. Many today see their experiences as the most important source of their beliefs.

However, stating that we use these four sources also leads to questions about which scriptures we use, or which tradition we follow. It was presented as an explanation of why people believe different things rather than as a way of coming to reliable answers, including of course the answer that we just can't say for certain.

I find it more constructive to consider four slightly different sources:

- Revelation
- Experience
- Reason and humility
- Other people

They became my equivalent of the "scientific method".

Revelation

A preacher once said that no matter how good a detective Hercule Poirot was, he could never find out about his creator, Agatha Christie, unless she wrote herself into one of her books. At the heart of Christian theology is the belief that God has revealed himself in our story, most significantly through Jesus.

As none of us are old enough to have seen Jesus in the flesh, our only access to this revelation is through it being handed down in the Christian tradition and the pages of the Bible, and through seeing its impact on our world. Different faiths also believe that God has revealed himself in different ways. To my mind, revelation must be a primary source for theology, but we have to use other sources in order to access this revelation. Our other sources help us to decide what is revelation, and what is not, and what that revelation might mean.

Experience

The other primary source we have for our theology is our experience of the world. However, our experiences by themselves cannot lead to reliable conclusions.

Throughout history people have come to conclusions about what God is like from their experience. In the pre-scientific world, it was only natural to conclude that God or gods were behind the unpredictable forces of nature. Our modern understanding has shown that science can explain much of what we see in the natural world without having to believe in God. The same experience of natural forces may now lead to disbelief in God.

As well as our experiences of the external world, we have internal experiences which may affect our theology. For instance, when I was ten years old, I tried to pray for the first time. I had volunteered to take part in my school's Parent Teacher Association production of *The Wind in the Willows*. They wanted children to be the assorted small animals, but they had so many volunteers that we were only needed for two out of the four nights that the play was being performed. I then found out that I would not be taking part on the night my parents and grandparents were coming. I had failed to listen at some point. I did not want to get in trouble, and so I tried praying to the God I had heard about in church. I had a sense that he "picked up the other end of the telephone". I then told my mother about the problem at school, and things did get sorted. I was the only child to take part on three nights. No proof at all of God's existence. But it was the start of a relationship in which I have seen countless prayers answered.

William Temple, a twentieth-century Archbishop of Canterbury, is supposed to have said: "When I pray, coincidences happen." Not all my prayers have been answered in the way I have wanted, but as I look back over the years, I have had many experiences of this kind which have strengthened my faith in God.

Reason and humility

Accounts of revelation in the Bible, and our experience of the world, cannot by themselves lead to reliable conclusions. As rational and perhaps cynical human beings we have to consider whether the experiences I have described above may have completely rational explanations. We have to weigh the arguments in favour of the existence of God, based on the existence of the Church and the Bible, against the arguments doubting the existence of God based on the problem of suffering. The Bible itself is a remarkably varied book, and we need to use our reason in order to interpret it and apply it in our world today. I use reason to try to discern what happened in Israel nearly 2,000 years ago, and to decide what might be God's revelation and what might be man-made speculation. This book is my attempt to explain logically what I believe, and areas of uncertainty I am still struggling with.

In television crime dramas, evidence is put together to decide who might have committed a crime under the headings "means", "motive" and "opportunity". Did they have access to a gun? Did they have a reason to kill? Could they have been there when the shot was fired? In a similar way, we have good evidence of what the earliest Christians taught. If they were telling lies, surely others would have shouted them down? Why would they make it up? What was in it for them?

In crime dramas, the plots frequently involve detectives charging the wrong suspect. As I write I am aware that I have changed my mind on some issues over the past thirty years. One of the most valuable parts of my reason is the knowledge that I can get things wrong. Reason, by its nature, must include humility, leading to the possibility of re-thinking issues, or re-examining the evidence.

As an engineer that humility is a great safeguard against disaster. For crucial questions we need to check and double check because we might be wrong. One of the best ways of showing that humility is to make good use of my final source.

Other people

As I said above, tradition is considered a source for our theology. Tradition in that sense is the cumulative wisdom, experiences and decisions of the Church over the last 2,000 years. However, there are many different strands to this tradition. Just as I can be wrong, so any particular strand of tradition might be wrong. And looking back at some parts of church history, it is clear that the Church has frequently got things wrong.

I am reluctant therefore to describe tradition as a source that is comparable to experience and revelation. But tradition does contain the combined wisdom and experience of many generations. To ignore all tradition would therefore be extraordinarily arrogant. Why should I be right and they be wrong?

Any conclusions I come to must be formed from a combination of revelation, experience and reason, but not just my own experience, reason and anything God might have revealed to me. I must listen to other people, including the great variety of people behind our traditions, and people who disagree with me.

I conclude, therefore, that revelation and experience are our primary sources for theology. Reason enables us to access and develop these sources, and to apply them to the questions we ask. And the reason and experience of other people should always be considered. It would be foolish to reject alternative views without understanding why they are held.

The Bible: the word of God?

In the above discussion, I have distinguished between the Bible and revelation. Revelation, in the sense I have used the word, is God's revelation of himself. If, as Christians believe, Jesus is God in human form, then Jesus' words and actions are revelation. A prophet who prefaces a statement with "The Lord says" is stating that the words they give are revelation. But in church on Sundays we regularly end our Bible readings with the phrase: "This is the word of the Lord." Thus it has been considered by many Christians that all the Bible is in some way revelation. This belief is based on words from 2 Timothy 3:16:

> All scripture is inspired by God and is useful for teaching, for reproof, for correction, and for training in righteousness.

However, using our reason, we cannot treat every part of scripture as revelation in a simplistic way. I was shocked to read a book that backed up an argument by quoting one of Job's friends. In the book of Job, Job's friends were rebuked by God for being wrong:

> My wrath is kindled against you and against your two friends; for you have not spoken of me what is right.
>
> *Job 42:7*

I agreed with the point being made in the book, but I don't think it should have been backed up by someone whose words were criticized by God.

What is the Bible? This is a question I will return to over the following chapters. We can say for certain that it is a collection of historical documents, giving insight into the beliefs and actions of the Jews and the Early Church. Thinking of my four sources for theology, it is a mixture of accounts of God's revelation, the experience of many people, and the combined wisdom and reason of many authors. Deciding that it is all, in some way, inspired by God is a step of faith that I will address later.

Starting from solid foundations

I did the Durham University degree in theology in my first two years of ordination training, and then in my final year studied the more practical subjects connected with being a vicar that were not covered by the university degree. These included Mission—in particular how we share our faith—and Ethics, which should have included sexual ethics. I did these courses with the three students who had done the university degree with me and half a dozen others, who had come to Durham for ordination training, having done theology degrees elsewhere.

These courses were not a great success. The problem was that we did not have a common understanding of how to approach the subjects. The majority of us were from a moderately evangelical background, but a couple of people came from very "liberal" backgrounds. We disagreed about how we should use the Bible, what authority it had, and how to interpret it. But because we had a course book to read and set topics to discuss, we didn't have a framework for going back to basics and discussing the foundations. It was frustrating and, I felt, a missed opportunity. In civil engineering terms it was like trying to build without foundations. Perhaps like building a car with half a team committed to making it environmentally friendly while the other half wanted it to go fast.

In the final chapters of this book I will grapple with some contemporary issues related to how we should live out our lives today—power, money, sex and global warming. However, please don't skip to those chapters without reading the foundations. The foundations are crucial for all that is built on them.

I will explain first how I have applied these four sources to the most fundamental question of theology: Does God exist? From there I will explain how my faith has developed around the questions of the authority and reliability of the Bible, who Jesus is and why did he die. It is only then that I feel able to address the more controversial issues. Thinking about it as I write, I can see that the levels of uncertainty expand as the tower gets higher, but the solid foundations mean that that is OK.

Being willing to change your mind

One of my memories of theological college was a lecture about how we interpret biblical texts. We were told that we all take our presuppositions to the text when we first read it. The question is whether our presuppositions dictate how we understand the text, or whether we give permission for the text to change our presuppositions. That is a good question for all our theology. Our normal experience of learning is that we build on past lessons. However, in a world where we disagree about so much, having the humility to admit that our presuppositions or former lessons might be wrong opens up the possibility of real learning.

The history of science is full of examples of conflict where people have not been willing to change their false beliefs. We once believed that the earth was flat. We once believed that the sun, the planets and all the stars went round the earth. In my own field, we once believed that metal broke because it got "tired", weakened by time. Hence the name "metal fatigue". Now we know that the metal breaks because of cracks growing. Engineering is safer as a result.

For many centuries, the Church taught that slavery was acceptable. I am glad we have changed our minds.

In the New Testament, Jesus' first followers were called disciples, rather than Christians. Disciples are by definition people who are learning, and therefore do not know all the answers. I hope I will always have the humility to be a disciple and be willing to change my mind.

PART 2

Building Foundations

CHAPTER 4

Does God Exist?

At the heart of Christianity is the belief that God not only exists, but that he intervenes in our world. He did not just set things up at the beginning of time. He does not merely operate in a spiritual dimension. He has intervened in our history.

This fundamental foundation of Christianity is in conflict with a world view that everything must have a scientific explanation. For most people in our secular age, this belief system is taught from childhood. It is the natural assumption behind teaching science. We have found the logical explanation for everything we see around us. We no longer believe that thunderbolts are from "gods". We know that they are caused by electrical charges built up in storm clouds. So there is a natural assumption that other apparently supernatural events must have a natural explanation.

I believe and trust the science I have learnt, but I also believe that God can intervene.

The crucial argument for my belief in the existence of God is that Jesus rose from the dead after he had been killed. I can find no scientific explanation for it. It is the foundation for my worldview that science cannot explain everything. It is the foundation for my faith and leaves my mind open to the possibility that other miracles might occur. It is fundamental to all that follows. Without the argument that Jesus rose from the dead, I would probably be an atheist.

Did Jesus rise from the dead?

As a teenager, at a grammar school where logic and intellectual rigour were held in high esteem, this was a key question. In those years I was influenced by the reasoning within two books: *Who Moved the Stone?* by Frank Morison,[6] and *Evidence that Demands a Verdict* by Josh McDowell.[7] These authors were lawyers who started off examining the historical evidence intending to prove that the resurrection did not happen. Instead they came to believe it. More recently, similar arguments were used in courses like *Alpha*. My version is as follows.

As I said in the introduction, in real science some things cannot be demonstrated in a laboratory. The theories of evolution and the Big Bang are theories because you cannot prove them in the way you can prove Newton's laws of motion. They were initially hypotheses which began by looking at how the world or universe is now, and then worked backwards in time to attempt to discover a cause.

Our telescopes show that the universe is expanding, and so it is logical to deduce that this expansion has been occurring for billions of years, from one initial point. From there, the theory of the Big Bang develops. It is the most logical explanation for all we can observe around us.

Fossils have been discovered in different layers of rocks showing that plants and animals have become more sophisticated or specialized over millions of years. Current observations show that genetics produce variation. It is logical that the variations most suited to successful reproduction are more likely to be passed to subsequent generations. We deduce the concept of survival of the fittest, which enables a species to adapt to its environment. The theory of evolution is a logical development of this concept. I am convinced.

In a similar way, I believe that the most logical explanation for the existence of the Christian faith today is that Jesus rose from the dead. I start with the fact that the Church exists today and try to work back. Why did it start?

There are vast numbers of historical documents that testify to the development of the Early Church, in particular the writings that were collected together and became our New Testament. In the libraries and museums of the world there are over 5,000 pieces of papyrus and vellum containing parts or all of these writings, with the earliest containing part of John's Gospel dating to 130 CE. F. F. Bruce comments that, in comparison, the earliest manuscripts of Caesar's *Gallic War* were written about 900 years after Caesar, yet no one questions their authenticity.[8]

We can be certain that Christians throughout the Roman Empire read and used the Gospels. Just as fossils tell us about life millions of years ago, so the manuscripts show us what Christians believed and taught in the Early Church. The consensus of the vast majority of scholars is that the Gospels were written between 60 and 110 CE. Mark's Gospel was almost certainly the earliest, written between 60 and 70 CE, just thirty or forty years after Jesus' public ministry and death.

The crucial point for me is that the Gospels were read, treasured and copied by the Early Church within living memory of the events of Jesus' public ministry and death. The Gospels state that Jesus died on the cross and rose again. If it was not true, why would the Gospels say it was? Why would the disciples make it up? Or could they have been deluded?

The leaders of the Early Church had little earthly reward for their leadership. They did not live in comfortable vicarages with a salary and pension like I do. Instead they risked persecution and death, especially under Emperor Nero. From the Acts of the Apostles we know that Stephen and James were both killed for their faith, and James was one of Jesus' inner circle of disciples. From later Christian writings, we know that Peter and Andrew, two other close disciples, were killed, as was Paul, who wrote many of the New Testament letters.

I can think of no reason why the disciples would have said that Jesus rose from the dead if it was not true. They had nothing to gain from the lie. If it were not true, they would have gone back to fishing, or whatever work they could get.

It has been suggested that Jesus didn't really die, but that he was taken down unconscious from the cross and then revived. But if Jesus didn't die, and simply recovered from his crucifixion, what happened to him afterwards? Why don't we read of his life after the crucifixion and his subsequent death years later? The Gospels are clear that Jesus did not come back to life in the way Lazarus was brought back from the dead. His resurrection left an empty tomb and a living body that was in some way different. He could enter a room when its doors were locked and then disappear again. He appeared to his disciples physically over a period of forty days before ascending into heaven. The exact nature of his resurrection is mysterious. It is outside our experience. But it was clearly not a resuscitation.

It has also been suggested that the disciples were deluded. That something about their grief made them imagine that Jesus rose from the dead. I cannot believe that either. The Gospel accounts of Jesus' resurrection all show the disciples as grieving, and then naturally doubting. Thomas in particular, in John's Gospel, declared that he would not believe it when the other disciples told him that Jesus was risen. Thomas stated that he would not believe unless he touched Jesus with his own hands. These are not accounts of mass hysteria. They are accounts of normal grieving people who took a lot of convincing.

There have, of course, been bishops who have declared that they cannot believe in the resurrection, and many Christians have lost their faith. However, that makes the point to me that believing is not easy. Why, if it were not true, would the Church have been started, and expanded so rapidly in the first century? Why did it not die within living memory of Jesus if it was based on the testimony of a few deluded souls?

The only argument against Jesus' resurrection that to me has any credibility is that Judas took Jesus' body as part of his remorse for betraying Jesus. He then committed suicide, leaving the disciples with an empty tomb. However, I cannot believe that an empty tomb alone would have been enough to convince the disciples that Jesus had risen. By itself the empty tomb would not have been enough for them to make up the details we read in the Gospels and then be willing to die for their faith.

In this country many people are now naturally sceptical about matters of faith, and anything that strikes them as supernatural. However, I think that healthy scepticism is also needed when reading newspapers or articles on the internet. When I was at Durham studying theology, the *Alpha* course was hitting the headlines. I read one article by a reporter who heard Nicky Gumbel, who developed the *Alpha* course, giving his arguments for why he believed Jesus rose from the dead. The journalist expressed his surprise, saying that no university professors of theology believed in the resurrection. At the time I was having lectures from my Head of Department, Professor James Dunn, who believed in the resurrection.⁹ It was the reporter, not Nicky, who was either ignorant or lying.

There are, I am sure, some professors of theology who don't believe in the resurrection. I hope we can all make our own minds up, by looking at the evidence and the arguments, not just believing someone because of their name, title or job.

I believe that Jesus rose from the dead. This one argument is crucial for my worldview, that God exists and has intervened in the world.

So why don't people believe?

In the paragraphs above I criticized a journalist for what I consider to be inaccurate reporting, which discouraged people from believing. However, I think a more significant reason many don't believe is inaccurate claims made about the Bible by some Christians. Including me.

When I was a teenager, a number of Christian leaders I knew proclaimed that the Bible was without error. In Luke's Gospel, Jesus heals Bartimaeus as he approaches Jericho.¹⁰ In Mark's Gospel, he heals him as they are leaving Jericho.¹¹ I remember a youth leader saying that this isn't a contradiction because there were two parts of Jericho, so you could be leaving one while approaching the other.

A few years later, when I was studying for my degree in engineering, I was in a hall of residence and my next-door neighbour was called Dave. In conversation, he said that the Bible was full of contradictions. I said that it wasn't. He asked to borrow my Bible and turned to Luke 24:4, which speaks of the disciples finding the empty tomb. Luke wrote:

> Suddenly two men in dazzling clothes stood beside them.

Then he turned to Mark 16:5:

> As they entered the tomb, they saw a young man, dressed in a white robe . . .

Dave's question was quite simple: were there two men dressed in white, or just one? He was a mathematician, but even to an engineer one and two are different numbers.

Anyone who reads the New Testament with an open and enquiring mind can find more of these inconsistencies. For example:

- According to John, Jesus' last words on the cross were, "It is finished",[12] but Luke states that his last words were, "Father into your hands I commit my spirit."[13]
- According to Matthew, Judas hanged himself,[14] but in Acts it says that he bought a field with his silver, fell into it and his body burst open.[15]

The belief in the "inerrancy of scripture" as defined by the Chicago statement was once a standard doctrine of some parts of the evangelical wing of the Church:

1. Holy Scripture, being God's own Word, written by men prepared and superintended by His Spirit, is of infallible divine authority in all matters upon which it touches: it is to be believed, as God's instruction, in all that it affirms; obeyed, as God's command, in all that it requires; embraced, as God's pledge, in all that it promises.
2. Being wholly and verbally God-given, Scripture is without error or fault in all its teaching, no less in what it states about God's acts in creation, about the events of world history, and about its own literary origins under God, than in its witness to God's saving grace in individual lives.
3. The authority of Scripture is inescapably impaired if this total divine inerrancy is in any way limited or disregarded, or made relative to a view of truth contrary to the Bible's own; and such lapses bring serious loss to both the individual and the Church.[16]

As a nineteen-year-old I signed declarations of faith for the Evangelical Alliance and my University Christian Union that affirmed this inerrancy of scripture. I now have to say that I think this doctrine is indefensible, as my neighbour at university pointed out to my embarrassment. The Bible has errors in the way normal human beings define error. For many people, the Bible is ignored or ridiculed, not because of minor contradictions that are to be expected in historical documents, but because of Christians who insist that it is inerrant.

Yet the Bible itself does not claim to be without error. In 2 Timothy 3:16 we read:

> All scripture is inspired by God and is useful for teaching, for reproof, for correction, and for training in righteousness.

I do believe that the Bible is inspired by God and useful. I have found that in many ways it has taught, trained and corrected me. But the Bible contains many accounts of God inspiring and working through imperfect people. To say that the Bible is without error either ignores what the Bible is, or redefines the word "error". It also means that we lose credibility with those who don't believe.

As Peter Enns wrote:

> I do not think that inerrancy can capture the Bible's varied character and complex dynamics. Though intended to protect the Bible, inerrancy actually sells it short . . . [17]

As thinking adults, considering matters of faith, we need to treat the Bible as it is, not what we might like it to be. The Bible is a significant collection of historical documents. It gives remarkable insights into the history of the Jewish people, the public ministry of Jesus and the development of the Early Church. That historicity provides a foundation for my faith that I am prepared to stake my life on. I do believe that it is more than just historical documents, but that belief is built on these historical foundations.

I am glad to say the current Evangelical Alliance statement of faith was changed and the word "inerrancy" removed. Instead it now declares belief in:

The divine inspiration and supreme authority of the Old and New Testament Scriptures, which are the written Word of God—fully trustworthy for faith and conduct.[18]

I will return to this in the following chapters.

Science and creationism

In today's world, the issue of whether the Bible has "errors" is highlighted in the media in connection with how the world was made. Some Christians, known as "creationists", believe that the world was made in six days, and that therefore the theories of the Big Bang and evolution are wrong. This is based on a literal reading of the account of creation in the first two chapters of Genesis. In the United States this has led to high-profile debates as to what schools are allowed to teach. Creationists hold the view not only that the Bible is inerrant, but also that the early chapters of Genesis have to be interpreted as literal history.[19]

I held that view when I was younger, arguing that God could arrange rocks and fossils to make the world look like it was billions of years old, when really it was much younger. Logically, if you believe in God, all things are possible.

However, in an RE lesson at school we compared Genesis 1 and Genesis 2. It was an eye-opener.

According to Genesis 1, on the third day the land produced vegetation of all kinds, and then on the sixth day God created all land-based creatures before finally creating men and women. But in Genesis 2:4–7 we read:

> In the day that the Lord God made the earth and the heavens, when no plant of the field was yet in the earth and no herb of the field had yet sprung up—for the Lord God had not caused it to rain upon the earth, and there was no one to till the ground; but a stream would rise from the earth, and water the whole face of the ground—then the Lord God formed man from the dust of the ground, and breathed into his nostrils the breath of life; and the man became a living being.

So according to Genesis 1, God makes all the vegetation on the third day, and men and women three days later. In Genesis 2, God makes a man before the plants have sprung up, and only makes a woman after the man has named all the animals, with none being a suitable partner for him. Simply comparing Genesis 1 and Genesis 2 shows clearly that they are not literal scientific history. As John Stott put it:

> We do not have to choose between Genesis 1 and contemporary cosmology or astrophysics. For the Bible was never intended by God to be a scientific textbook. Indeed, it should be evident to readers that Genesis 1 is a highly stylized and beautiful poem. Both accounts of creation (scientific and poetic) are true, but they are given from different perspectives and are complementary to one another.[20]

However, the high profile that Creationist Christians have had in the media might make people think that the Bible is not to be taken seriously.

I believe in the theories of evolution and the Big Bang, and I don't see them as being in conflict with the Bible. I consider the New Testament to be a collection of historical documents that provide a solid foundation for my faith. But I do not believe the Bible is without error in the way the world normally defines error. I do believe the Bible is inspired and useful in teaching, training and correcting us, but that we need to be cautious in our interpretation.

What about suffering?

While the arguments for the existence of God outlined above are, in my mind, conclusive, there are also powerful arguments for atheism, the belief that God does not exist, based on the observation of suffering in the world.

When I was studying for my degree in theology, we read part of *The Brothers Karamazov*. In the following passage, Ivan speaks of one appalling moment of suffering, and his struggle in response:

A serf-boy, a little child of eight, threw a stone in play and hurt the paw of the general's favorite hound. 'Why is my favorite dog lame?' He is told that the boy threw a stone that hurt the dog's paw. 'So you did it.' The general looked the child up and down. 'Take him.' He was taken—taken from his mother and kept shut up all night. Early that morning the general comes out on horseback, with the hounds, his dependents, dog-boys, and huntsmen, all mounted around him in full hunting parade. The servants are summoned for their edification, and in front of them all stands the mother of the child. The child is brought from the lock-up. It's a gloomy, cold, foggy autumn day, a capital day for hunting. The general orders the child to be undressed; the child is stripped naked. He shivers, numb with terror, not daring to cry . . . . 'Make him run,' commands the general. 'Run! run!' shout the dog-boys. The boy runs . . . . 'At him!' yells the general, and he sets the whole pack of hounds on the child. The hounds catch him, and tear him to pieces before his mother's eyes! . . .

Tell me yourself, I challenge you—answer. Imagine that you are creating a fabric of human destiny with the object of making men happy in the end, giving them peace and rest at last, but that it was essential and inevitable to torture to death only one tiny creature—that baby beating its breast with its fist, for instance—and to found that edifice on its unavenged tears, would you consent to be the architect on those conditions?[21]

More recently, Stephen Fry expressed similar sentiments when Irish TV presenter Gay Byrne asked what he would say to God if he died and had to confront him. Fry's reply was:

How dare you create a world in which there is such misery that is not our fault? It's not right. It's utterly, utterly evil. Why should I respect a capricious, mean-minded, stupid God who creates a world which is so full of injustice and pain? . . . I would say: 'bone cancer in children? What's that about?'[22]

As a vicar I have taken hundreds of funerals, including some for babies, for children, and for young parents who were leaving children without a mum or a dad. I remember listening to one distraught mother talking about how she prayed for God to save her son, and yet he died. As a result, she said she could no longer believe in God.

To believe in a God who is all-powerful and all-loving can seem impossible in the face of such suffering. For many people "God's only excuse is that he doesn't exist".

The Bible has wrestled with the issue, without giving what I would call an answer. The book of Job is the story of a devout man who is portrayed as doing nothing wrong. In chapter 1 God declares about Job:

> There is no one like him on the earth, a blameless and upright man who fears God and turns away from evil.

But then God allows Satan to test Job, so that Job's children are killed, all his wealth taken from him and he is left on a rubbish heap covered in painful sores.

The following chapters are a debate between Job and his so-called friends about the cause of his suffering. His friends state that Job must have done something to deserve it, while Job maintains his innocence. In the end, God puts Job's friends in their place and renews Job's prosperity, but he never gives an answer as to why he allows suffering, except to say that it is clearly not a punishment for sin.

Like the Bible's accounts of creation, I don't think Job is meant to be literal history. It seems unlikely that God and Satan have conversations as described in Job 1. Instead, like the parables Jesus taught, the book of Job is a story that sums up and wrestles with the truth and problem of suffering in our world.

In preparing to write this book, I also read C. S. Lewis' *A Grief Observed* in which Lewis describes, with extraordinary honesty, his thoughts and emotions following his wife's death from cancer. In his grief he describes God as a cosmic sadist. In the end he can only conclude that somehow suffering is necessary, though we cannot understand why. He compares us with animals suffering at the hands of a vet, where the surgery is necessary, but makes no sense to the animal. In the end Lewis's faith is renewed, but his questions are unanswered. He senses that God is gazing at him with compassion, perhaps shaking his head, as a father would in comforting a child who can't understand.[23]

My belief

In spite of my concern about suffering, I am convinced that Jesus rose from the dead. If it were not true, I cannot think why the Church would have started. As a consequence, I believe that God does exist, and does intervene in our world. That is the foundation on which the following chapters build. I still struggle with the question of why God allows so much suffering in the world, and it is a question I will return to, not just in this book, but throughout my life.

CHAPTER 5

How Reliable Are the Gospels?

In the last chapter I explained why I believe in Jesus' resurrection based on treating the New Testament as historical documents. I am convinced that the documents show that from the very beginning the Church taught that Jesus died and rose again. I cannot think why they would have made it up when they had nothing to gain from the lie.

However, I also argued that the Gospels were not without error. In this chapter I will recount more of my journey, as I considered how reliable the Gospels are, and to what extent they make a solid foundation for what follows. Like the foundations of a building, this chapter may not be exciting, but I believe it is vital.

Diversity of opinions

While doing research as an engineer before I was ordained, I was also doing a training course to become a Church of England reader. Readers, like lay preachers in other churches, are authorized to preach and lead worship in the Church of England. The first essay I had to write was on the question, "What was Jesus' attitude to the Jewish Law?". I mentioned the essay question to a friend who had studied theology at Oxford. She asked me what I was reading for it, and I innocently answered, "the Bible". She expressed horror, saying that there were too many difficulties: how could I try to answer the question from the Bible alone? She recommended that I read a book by one of her professors—E. P. Sanders' *Jesus and Judaism*.

I was at first glad of the advice, because I had found the Bible confusing. For instance, in Matthew 5:17, 18:

> Do not think that I have come to abolish the law or the prophets; I have come not to abolish but to fulfil. For truly I tell you, until heaven and earth pass away, not one letter, not one stroke of a letter, will pass from the law until all is accomplished.

It seems clear from this verse that Jesus had not come to abolish the law. Yet the Early Church stopped obeying the laws on circumcision and diet. Were they ignoring Jesus' statement?

I turned to Sanders' book in the hope of finding some answers. Instead a chasm of uncertainty opened up before me. Concerning the verses I was struggling with, Sanders simply stated that Jesus never said them. He didn't give an explanation in that chapter as to why he believed that Jesus didn't say those words.[24] At that point, with an essay to write, I put the book down and used more conservative resources. But with that encounter my eyes were opened to many questions that I needed to return to about the reliability of the New Testament. I started that journey on my readers' training course and continued it in my theology degree and in reading and writing for this book.

During my studies in theology at Durham, I discovered that Sanders' work was part of a major theological reassessment of who Jesus was. It was connected with the realization that many inherited depictions of Jesus were frankly wrong. In the stained-glass windows in my church, Jesus is shown with white skin and blond hair. But he was a Jew, born in Israel! Some phrases in our Christmas carols are nothing but Victorian brainwashing: there is no evidence that little Lord Jesus didn't cry, and describing him as mild and obedient is not compatible with Jesus driving moneychangers out of the temple. Perhaps more seriously, in our Sunday School lessons and church sermons, Jesus' background and culture as a first-century Jew had been almost entirely ignored.

From an engineer's point of view, this reassessment struck me as a good thing. Surely we should check what we believe, and have the humility to think that we might be wrong. However, initially it felt frightening, suggesting that the "facts" that I had based my faith on might not be true. As I wrote above, it has to be wise to listen to people who disagree with us, if we want to work out the truth. It can also be uncomfortable. In case any reader is scared to continue, in the end, nothing in my studies in Durham left me questioning the foundations of my faith. I am still convinced that Jesus died on the cross and rose again. My personal reassessment in the end gave me a firmer historical foundation for the core of what I believe, while also showing me that some "facts" I had taken for granted were open to debate.

Biblical criticism

In reassessing who Jesus was, the first logical step to consider is how reliable the New Testament is and, in particular, how reliable the Gospels are as historical accounts of Jesus' life and ministry. Biblical criticism is a broad term for the discipline of examining the biblical texts and ancient evidence, including their age and historical accuracy. Biblical criticism sounds like a threatening phrase if you treasure the Bible. However, healthy criticism can be constructive, separating the wheat from the chaff. Those who trust that the Gospels are divinely inspired should not be afraid of examining their historical basis. In metallurgical terms, gold does not get destroyed in fire, but any impurities will rise to the surface.

As I explained in my introduction, we develop our theology from four sources: revelation, experience, reason and other people. As the Bible was written many centuries ago, in languages that most of us cannot read, most of us can only access this primary source of revelation by using the accumulated reason and experience—and the dedicated hard work—of others. The disciplines of forensic science are used to try to look back in time and discover the facts about a crime, including the uncertainties. In a similar way, I found the disciplines of biblical criticism helped me to look back in time and give me a clearer picture of the foundational events of my faith.

For my generation of evangelical Christians, the most influential scholarly book on the reliability of the New Testament documents was F. F. Bruce's *The New Testament Documents: Are They Reliable?*[25] Professor Bruce was the Rylands Professor of Biblical Criticism and Exegesis at the University of Manchester. He introduced me, and many others, to the topic and in particular to some of the ancient manuscripts that provide evidence for their reliability.

At Durham I began looking at the evidence for myself and was exposed to a greater breadth of scholarship. F. F. Bruce would be considered "conservative", someone whose conclusions suggested a greater age and reliability to the New Testament documents. Sanders, mentioned above, would be considered more "critical", tending to greater scepticism. Growing up within the evangelical wing of the Church, I had conservative writers recommended to me. They mostly confirmed or built upon what I had previously learned. They didn't challenge me to consider the foundations, or to examine whether some of my presuppositions were false. At the moment, I am trying to buy a house for my future retirement. Before buying it, we are having a survey done, and I want the surveyor to be critical, to find anything that might be wrong with the foundations or the structure before I am committed to buying it. So too, for my faith: I want to know if I am building on solid foundations. If I am, then there is no problem with examining them again. If I am not, I need to re-examine and re-lay them, or I am at risk of getting other doctrines wrong.

To be more up-to-date for writing this book, I have also used Delbert Burkett's *Introduction to the New Testament and the Origins of Christianity*.[26] This is a more modern summary of the subject, from someone who is on the critical side compared to F. F. Bruce.

In support of this I have also enjoyed reading some of the ancient documents themselves, now available in translation at <http://www.earlychristianwritings.com/>.

I could write at great length on the subject of the reliability of the New Testament, but if you want to go deeper, I recommend you read the above resources for yourself. Instead, here are the main pieces of evidence and conclusions that have been significant for me.

Who wrote the Gospels and when were they written?

Mark's Gospel
Papias, Bishop of Hierapolis, wrote between 100 and 140 CE:

> Mark having become the interpreter of Peter, wrote down accurately whatsoever he remembered. It was not, however, in

exact order that he related the sayings or deeds of Christ. For he neither heard the Lord nor accompanied Him. But afterwards, as I said, he accompanied Peter, who accommodated his instructions to the necessities [of his hearers], but with no intention of giving a regular narrative of the Lord's sayings. Wherefore Mark made no mistake in thus writing some things as he remembered them. For of one thing he took especial care, not to omit anything he had heard, and not to put anything fictitious into the statements.[27]

Mark, the Gospel author according to Papias, is thought to be John Mark, mentioned in the New Testament as travelling with Barnabas and Paul, and later in life being a great help to Paul (Acts 12:12; 2 Timothy 4:11). In addition, 1 Peter 5:13 includes Peter sending greetings from "my son Mark". So according to Papias, this Mark wrote the Gospel from the eyewitness accounts of Peter the apostle. F. F. Bruce suggests a date of 64 CE.[28]

Supporting evidence for Mark as the author comes from Ireneaus, written around 175 CE:

Mark, the disciple and interpreter of Peter, did also hand down to us in writing what had been preached by Peter.[29]

Reading more "critical" authors shows that Mark's role in the Gospel is not universally accepted. Delbert Burkett states that most "critical scholars" doubt Papias' claim that Mark's Gospel is based on Peter's preaching. His argument is that there are other instances of writings of that time falsely attributed to the apostles or other authority figures.[30]

In the previous chapter, I argued that there was no logical reason for the disciples to invent or falsify accounts of the resurrection. In the case of Irenaeus and Papias there were reasons why they might have wanted to give a greater authority to the four Gospels in our Bibles. In the second century, heretical views began to arise in the Church, especially in the form of Gnosticism. Gnostic teachers supported their claims with Gospels attributed to other apostles. To counter those claims, attributing the four Gospels included in our Bibles to an apostle would make sense. However, if that was the case why choose Mark rather than Peter himself?

Mark's authorship cannot be proved beyond all doubt. However, Burkett still agrees that Mark is an edited collection of the oral traditions on the life of Jesus, handed down from the apostles. Burkett suggests a date of 70 CE for Mark's Gospel.

Scholars can argue about the strength of the arguments for Mark's authorship and for the earlier or later date. For me the evidence is enough to trust Mark's Gospel as an accurate portrayal of what was being taught in the Church within forty years of Jesus' death. I can still remember major events from my life from fifty years ago. I can remember the names of nearly everyone in my class from when I started at secondary school forty-four years ago. I have spoken to many people in their eighties who can clearly recall events from their childhood. If Mark's Gospel were not an accurate portrayal of the main events and teaching of Jesus' public ministry, why would he make it up? And why would it have been accepted by the Church?

A friend, on reading a draft of this chapter, said that it felt rather heavy and scholarly. My apologies if it feels like that, but reading Richard Dawkins' *The God Delusion* convinced me of the need for proper, referenced scholarly work. In his argument against the Gospels being a reliable foundation for belief in God, Dawkins states:

> Ever since the nineteenth century, scholarly theologians have made an overwhelming case that the gospels are not reliable accounts of what happened in the history of the real world. All were written long after the death of Jesus... All were then copied and recopied, through many different "Chinese Whispers generations" by fallible scribes who, in any case, had their own religious agendas.[31]

However, Dawkins does not reference the theologians, or give details of those who might give counter arguments. And yet the English version of Dawkins' book has sold over three million copies.[32]

Matthew's and Luke's Gospels
Papias also wrote about Matthew:

> Matthew put together the oracles [of the Lord] in the Hebrew language, and each one interpreted them as best he could.[33]

Irenaeus wrote:

> Matthew also issued a written Gospel among the Hebrews in their own dialect.[34]

It is unlikely that Papias and Irenaeus are referring to Matthew's Gospel as we have it now, but it is strong evidence that Matthew the apostle did produce a written account of Jesus' words. As Greek was the dominant language of the Church, it is not surprising that the Hebrew original was not widely copied and circulated, but F. F. Bruce suggests that it is likely to have been a source used in compiling the Gospels.[35]

Source criticism

Source criticism seeks to identify the sources used in compiling the Gospels. When we compare Matthew, Mark and Luke's Gospels some passages in them are almost identical. Matthew and Luke are thought to have copied large parts of Mark and added material from other sources. The material in Matthew and Luke that is not in Mark has been given the name Q. F. F. Bruce suggested that Matthew's collection of Jesus' words may have been Q: the differences between the Greek of Q passages in Matthew and Luke can be explained as different translations from a Hebrew/Aramaic source.

In addition, Matthew and Luke each have unique material, suggesting further individual sources.

Redaction criticism

Redaction criticism is the study of how the Gospel writers edited their material, and perhaps altered it, to suit their own audiences and possibly their own agendas. For example, Mark 7:3 explains that the Pharisees did not eat until after they had ceremonially washed. This indicates that Mark was expecting his Gospel to be read by people who were not familiar with Jewish customs.

More significantly, going back to where I started this chapter, trying to write an essay on Jesus and his attitude to the law, it was suggested that the author of Matthew put words on Jesus' lips that were not his. In Matthew 5:17, 18:

> Do not think that I have come to abolish the law or the prophets; I have come not to abolish but to fulfil. For truly I tell you, until heaven and earth pass away, not one letter, not one stroke of a letter, will pass from the law until all is accomplished.

One of the great controversies of the Early Church was the extent to which they should follow the Jewish law. Matthew's Gospel is thought to have been written for a primarily Jewish audience, probably from a part of the Church that held the law in high esteem. It is therefore argued that the author of Matthew's Gospel added or changed the words Jesus used to reflect his theological position.

However, Luke 16:17 has Jesus saying:

> It is easier for heaven and earth to pass away, than for one stroke of a letter in the law to be dropped.

I am not convinced by the argument. According to Acts, Luke was a companion of Paul and Paul was a primary advocate of setting aside the law.

From my conservative background the idea of the Gospel writers inventing or distorting Jesus' words to suit their own agendas is quite a shock. But if Jesus did say the words quoted in Matthew 5 concerning keeping the law, then what did he mean?

Going back to my engineer's approach to theology, I have to acknowledge that there are some things we do not know. I am convinced that Matthew, Mark and Luke all reflect the teaching of the Early Church within living memory of the events of Jesus' public ministry. Scholars agree that Mark was written between 64 and 70 CE. Matthew and Luke are thought to have been written between 70 and 100 CE, and Luke was a companion of Paul on some of his travels. For me this is a good reason to trust these texts as a reliable account of the main events and teaching of Jesus' public ministry. They are clearly not "without error" in the minor details. I acknowledge the argument that the author of Matthew might have made changes to Jesus' teaching to reflect his own theological view of the law. I am not convinced by the argument, but treating the Gospels as historical documents, we have to admit to areas of uncertainty. Those areas do not affect the core of my faith.

John's Gospel

John's Gospel is thought to be the latest of the Gospels to be written, between 80 and 110 CE. F. F. Bruce states that Ignatius of Antioch was influenced by the teaching of the Gospel, and he was martyred around 115 CE.[36] In addition, a fragment of papyrus containing John 18:31–33 and 37 was found in Egypt, and this has been dated to between 125 and 150 CE.[37]

The Gospel itself names the beloved disciple, probably John, as the eyewitness behind the events it relates:

> This is the disciple who is testifying to these things and has written them, and we know that his testimony is true.
>
> *John 21:24*

The fact that this verse says the disciple wrote the events down suggests that either he was the author of the Gospel, or that he was the author of a source which others used. The "we" in John 21:24 suggests that others were involved in its compilation in some way.

External evidence of John the Disciple being the author is given again by Irenaeus in around 175 CE:

> Afterwards, John, the disciple of the Lord, who also had leaned upon His breast, did himself publish a Gospel during his residence at Ephesus in Asia.[38]

However, Burkett states that most modern scholars doubt that John was the author.[39] The grounds for this are:

1. A lack of evidence that John ever lived in Ephesus, whereas there is evidence for Paul's time there.
2. Some evidence that John was martyred around 70 CE.
3. The fact that the theology in John is much more "advanced" than Matthew, Mark and Luke. Its introduction, for instance, states that Jesus was in the beginning, and all things were made through him.

All I can conclude is that, historically speaking, we cannot say with any degree of certainty who the author of the fourth Gospel was. However, we do know that it must have been written by 110 CE, and that it was accepted by the Early Church.

Did God really say . . . ? Creative writing?

The question that most arises from comparing John's Gospel with the others is why the Gospels don't all contain the same incidents and teaching, although there is obviously a good deal of overlap.

For many Christians, some of the most well-known words of Jesus are:

I am the bread of life (John 6:35).

I am the light of the world (John 8:12).

I am the good shepherd (John 10:11).

I am the resurrection and the life (John 11:25).

I am the way, and the truth, and the life (John 14:6).

But these are only found in John's Gospel. If Jesus said them, why didn't the other Gospel writers record them?

The same question arises for the parables of the Good Samaritan and the Prodigal Son. Why are they only in Luke?

It is of course possible that the different apostles or Gospel authors had different parables or sayings that were their favourites, and they chose them for particular audiences. Matthew included parables warning of judgement for his Jewish audience, who were in danger of missing their Messiah. Luke might have included parables that speak of God's mercy, seeking the lost sheep and welcoming the lost son, because he was a companion of the apostle Paul, and Paul was very aware of his own sin. John's Gospel itself ends by saying that the author had to be selective in compiling the Gospel, leaving out vast amounts of Jesus' ministry.[40]

An alternative explanation, which I find uncomfortable, is that some of the writing in the Gospels is not the words that Jesus said, but the creative construction of Early Church preachers used to explain who Jesus was and his teaching.

I can remember many of the stories told by my vicar from when I was a young child. Because I have read the Bible, it is easy for me to know which of the stories that he told came from the Bible and which are from elsewhere. However, I have heard people who have assumed that the seven deadly sins are from the Bible. Similarly, I was once given a wonderful reading said to have come from Nelson Mandela, only to discover later that he was not the author. It was still an inspiring reading, and it was consistent with Mandela's teaching.

But what does that mean for my faith? If I admit the possibility that John put the "I am" sayings in Jesus' mouth, or if another preacher created the Parable of the Prodigal Son, does my faith come crashing down? The answer is no. Even with this uncertainty, the Gospels must contain the main points of Jesus' life and teaching, with any additions being creative extra explanations of the truth. As a vicar, when I am retelling a Bible story to children, I do not feel constrained to use the exact text of the Bible: instead, I try to communicate its truth in a way that will engage them. For generations, children have been taught that Mary and Joseph went to Bethlehem on a donkey, even though the Gospels make no mention of one.

The key point for my faith is that the Gospels were accepted without any record of significant dispute by the Early Church, as a summary of the disciples' teaching about Jesus. I can think of no reason for the disciples or early preachers to have substantially changed the teaching or events, though they may have been creative in communicating that truth. Their priorities would have been spiritual and moral, rather than geographical, numerical, or chronological.

That foundation for my faith is further strengthened by the Early Church's debate as to which books should be considered orthodox, and in time included in what is our New Testament.

The Early Church's debate on the New Testament canon

As I said above, the Gospels were accepted by the Early Church, and there is no record of any dispute as to their truthfulness in the ancient documents. However, in the second century, there were significant disputes when gathering together a collection of documents to be considered essential for the Early Church. This collection became our New Testament. The debate was connected with two significant "heresies": teaching that was considered to be incompatible with orthodox teaching.

Marcionism

The first heresy was Marcionism. Marcion preached a form of Christianity that rejected the whole of the Old Testament, and all the teaching of a God who brings judgement. Marcion proposed a restricted list of scripture consisting of just the Gospel of Luke, and ten letters of Paul. In addition, he even wanted to delete some passages from Luke that he did not agree with.

Gnosticism

Gnosticism involved belief in additional teaching that was not contained in the Gospels, and was supported by documents said to have been written by the apostles or other authority figures. One of the better-known Gnostic works is the Gospel of Thomas. This consists of numerous sayings attributed to Jesus, many of which are in accord with Matthew, Mark, Luke and John. However, it includes extra words, speaking of hidden truths and hinting at routes to special religious experiences. For example:

These are the hidden words that the living Jesus spoke. And Didymus Judas Thomas wrote them down.

13: Jesus said to his disciples: "Compare me, and tell me whom I am like." Simon Peter said to him: "You are like a just messenger." Matthew said to him: "You are like an (especially) wise philosopher." Thomas said to him: "Teacher, my mouth will not bear at all to say whom you are like." Jesus said: "I am not your teacher. For you have drunk, you have become intoxicated at the bubbling spring that I have measured out." And he took him, (and) withdrew, (and) he said three words to him. But when Thomas came back to his companions, they asked him: "What did Jesus say to you?" Thomas said to them: "If I tell you one of the words he said to me, you will pick up stones and throw them at me, and fire will come out of the stones (and) burn you up."

114: Simon Peter said to them: "Let Mary go away from us, for women are not worthy of life." Jesus said: "Look, I will draw her in so as to make her male, so that she too may become a living male spirit, similar to you." (But I say to you): "Every woman who makes herself male will enter the kingdom of heaven."[41]

I found reading them both fascinating and worrying. The hidden and secretive nature of Gnosticism is obvious to see, as is the promotion of Thomas as a special disciple.

Agreeing the canon of the New Testament
The Early Church responded to these heresies by starting the process of agreeing which books were to be considered orthodox. In this process there were three main criteria that had to be satisfied for inclusion in the list:[42]

- Were they "orthodox"? That is, did the book conform to the traditional teaching of the Church? Saying this immediately shows that the Church had a sense of what was orthodox teaching, widely accepted in the diverse geography of the Church.
- Did they have apostolic origin? They were concerned that the teaching about Jesus should have come from those who knew

Jesus. In this respect Paul is also treated as an apostle, because of his special calling and foundational role, but of course he did not write a Gospel.

- Were they widely accepted? The orthodox books had arisen when the Church was much younger, and had spread with the Church. The newer and potentially heretical books might have adherents in one region, but would not be widely accepted.

I find it reassuring that the leaders of the Early Church were as concerned as I am for ascertaining what was true.

Given the evangelical view of scripture I was brought up with, it is also interesting that the Early Church did not ask the question of whether the writing was divinely inspired. The scriptures were a record of what the apostles said and taught, rather than a declaration that the words were "the word of God".

The first list for which we have documentary evidence is known as the Muratorian Canon, from a fragment of papyrus dated to around 175 CE. In this the writer states that they accepted all of the books in our New Testament except Hebrews, James, 1 and 2 Peter, and possibly one letter of John. These were disputed at the time. In addition, the author accepted the Apocalypse of Peter, though noting that some disputed it, and comments that the Shepherd of Hermas may be read as helpful but not authoritative. Concerning the accepted books he wrote:

> ... these are hallowed in the esteem of the Catholic Church, and in the regulation of ecclesiastical discipline. There are also in circulation one to the Laodiceans, and another to the Alexandrians, forged under the name of Paul, and addressed against the heresy of Marcion; and there are also several others which cannot be received into the Catholic Church, for it is not suitable for gall to be mingled with honey.[43]

A century later Church historian Eusebius states that the accepted list had become all of the books in our New Testament, except that James, Jude, 2 Peter, and 2 and 3 John were accepted by the majority of the Church, although some had reservations. Revelation split opinions.[44]

In the early fourth century, the Church was still suffering periodic persecution, and travel and communication were of course much more difficult than today. It was not until after Emperor Constantine became a Christian in 312 CE that bishops from the entire Church were able to gather, and the list of books in our New Testament was finalized in 393 CE.

In the light of the above I am content to accept that the books of our New Testament reflect the teaching of the Early Church in the first generation after Jesus' resurrection, and that provides a sure foundation upon which to build my theology. In saying that, I also acknowledge that there is some uncertainty around the edges. The unique features of some of the Gospels suggest that it is not unreasonable to believe that the Gospel writers or the sources used by them may have been creative in communicating the truth that Jesus taught. However, as far as I can understand, these disputed parts must be in accord with what is not disputed about Jesus.

The debate around John's Gospel, and his more explicit declaration of Jesus' divinity is, however, an issue for some. I will return to that in chapter 7.

Before that, one further area of biblical criticism. I have written about the dating, authorship and reliability of the New Testament documents. A final question is whether the New Testament we have now is the same as that written by its original authors, or whether it has been changed over the centuries. For that we use textual criticism.

Textual criticism—do we have the original texts?

Textual criticism seeks to discover the original text of each part of the Bible. We do not have the original manuscripts written by Matthew, Mark, Luke and John, but we have thousands of pieces of papyrus and vellum dating from 130 CE onwards. The original documents would have been written on papyrus which would have disintegrated with use. In order to share the documents, they were copied, and then copies made of the copies. There are some discrepancies in the text, where we assume mistakes have been made in copying it. This is not surprising! Textual criticism seeks to discern what the original text was.

Textual criticism uses two guidelines for when there are variations of a text in the different manuscripts:

- Firstly, the original text is more likely to be in the oldest manuscript, or the text found in manuscripts from a greater variety of places.
- Secondly, the original text is more likely to be the more "difficult text".

By difficult text, the scholars mean a text that one could imagine a copier wanting to change or water down. An example that illustrates this is from Luke 23:34, where Jesus is being crucified. In the normal text we read:

> Jesus said: "Father, forgive them, for they do not know what they are doing."

The footnote says that some ancient manuscripts do not have this sentence. The argument for keeping the sentence starts with the fact that the Early Church was persecuted by the Jewish and then the Roman authorities. The Early Church would therefore have had every reason to be bitter towards those who combined to kill Jesus and were now continuing that persecution. Jesus' prayer that his Father would forgive them is therefore a challenging phrase. Why would a Christian suffering persecution add it? So almost certainly Jesus' prayer for the forgiveness of his killers was part of the original text.

Following the process of textual criticism, the minor discrepancies where the text is uncertain are detailed in the footnotes of most Bibles. For example, in Luke 8:26 the normal text says that Jesus sailed to the region of the Gerasenes, but the footnote says that some manuscripts say Gadarenes, and others Gergesenes. These minor discrepancies in no way change the overall meaning of the text. The issue of whether Jesus prayed for forgiveness for those who killed him is more significant, but as Jesus commanded us to love our enemies in the Sermon on the Mount, it does not amount to a significant change to Jesus' teaching.

The conclusion of all the textual criticism of the New Testament is that the vast majority of the Greek text from which our Bibles are translated is an authentic record of what the original authors wrote.

There are just two more substantial discrepancies in the manuscripts. The first concerns John 8:1–11, where Jesus is presented with a woman caught in adultery and asked whether she should be stoned as prescribed in the Law of Moses. Jesus responds by saying:

> "Let anyone among you who is without sin be the first to throw a stone at her."

Of course, no one then throws a stone. The footnotes say that the earliest manuscripts do not include the story. C. K. Barrett states that the verses are also found in one ancient manuscript of Luke, and that it is unlikely to have been a part of the original Gospel, but that scribes must have added it from another ancient source.[45] So there is no reason to doubt the authenticity of the story, but it was probably not part of the original Gospel.

The second significant textual variation concerns the end of Mark's Gospel. Verses 9 to 20 of chapter 16 are not in the earliest manuscripts. Reading chapter 16 as a whole including the extra verses reveals a discontinuity at the end of verse 8. The chapter starts with the women finding Jesus' tomb empty, meeting an angel who tells them that Jesus had risen, and not telling anyone because they were afraid. Then at verse 9 it is as if the chapter starts again, with the statement that Jesus first appeared to Mary Magdalene, and a summary of Jesus' resurrection appearances. I understand that the style of the Greek also changes for these final verses.

It seems likely, therefore, that the extra verses were added at a later date. The best guess is that Mark was not able to finish his Gospel, perhaps because of being arrested as part of Nero's persecution of the Church. The extra verses were added so that the account was not left in mid-air, but not by Mark.

I am content to trust that the vast majority of the Greek New Testament that we have is what the original authors wrote, with the few minor uncertainties listed above.

Conclusion

My journey through the world of biblical criticism has at times been uncomfortable. I have realized that my presupposition of the New Testament as being "without error" is not correct. However, in the end my personal faith has been strengthened by all I have studied. To go back to my engineering analogy, biblical criticism, like a house survey, has confirmed for me that my faith rests on solid foundations. It has helped me to see that the Gospels reflect the life and teaching of Jesus and the Early Church to a level of proof I would risk my life upon. The early Christians risked their lives on it. Why would they make it up?

Combining Reason and Faith—God's sovereignty over scripture?

To summarize my conclusions from the last two chapters, I do believe that Jesus rose from the dead, and that therefore God exists and intervenes in our world. I also trust the New Testament, with the minimal reservations mentioned above. Putting these two conclusions together I trust that God has in some way overseen the writing and collection of the New Testament to give us the scripture we need. That does not mean it is without error. In the New Testament Jesus clearly shows that he can work through humans who make plenty of errors. Having worked through this review of the foundations of my faith, I am content to concentrate on engaging with the New Testament as we have it, putting it into action in my life, rather than continually reading and submerging myself in areas where we cannot be certain.

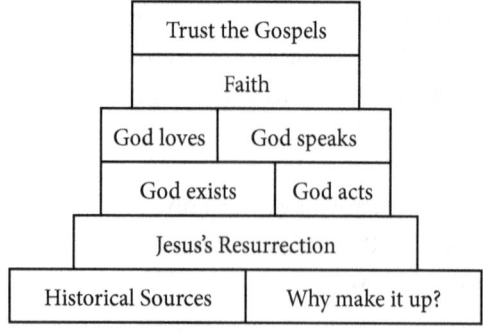

CHAPTER 6

What about the Old Testament? Treasure or Texts of Terror?

In the previous chapters I have explained the foundations for my faith, building up from the historical sources for the New Testament, and the question of "why would the Early Church make things up?"

Because I am convinced that Jesus died and was raised from the dead, I deduce that God not only exists, but has also chosen to act in this world. He loves. He speaks. Because of this I have faith in him, and I trust that he has in some way overseen the production of the New Testament to give me the truth I need to know.

However, what about the Old Testament? Paul wrote in his second letter to Timothy:

> All scripture is inspired by God and is useful for teaching, for reproof, for correction, and for training in righteousness.
>
> *2 Timothy 3:16*

The scripture Paul is referring to is of course the Old Testament. Many parts of the Old Testament are treasured by Christians. For example, Psalm 23, "The Lord is my Shepherd", is used at many Christian funerals, and the accounts of Abraham, Joseph, Moses, Elijah and many more have been significant in my faith journey.

But Deuteronomy 7:1–2 reads:

> When the Lord your God brings you into the land that you are about to enter and occupy, and he clears away many nations before you—the Hittites, the Girgashites, the Amorites, the

> Canaanites, the Perizzites, the Hivites, and the Jebusites, seven nations mightier and more numerous than you—and when the Lord your God gives them over to you and you defeat them, then *you must utterly destroy them*. [my italics]

Since I was a teenager, I have been shocked and confused by this genocidal instruction. I thought God commanded us to love our enemies? Walter Moberly, in his *Old Testament Theology*, writes:

> Here we face what may be the quintessential enigma and challenge of the Old Testament. One moment we are considering the mystery and wonder of divine love as fundamental to the calling and choosing of Israel; the next moment we are considering such choosing as a basis for apparent divinely-sponsored genocide. One moment we see God as loving; the next moment we see a deity who apparently sponsors mass murder. How should this be approached and understood?[46]

Richard Dawkins, in *The God Delusion*, states:

> The God of the Old Testament is arguably the most unpleasant character in all fiction: jealous and proud of it; a petty, unjust, unforgiving control-freak; a vindictive, bloodthirsty ethnic cleanser; a misogynistic, homophobic, racist, infanticidal, genocidal, filicidal, pestilential, megalomaniacal, sadomasochistic, capriciously malevolent bully.[47]

So-called New Atheists, of which Dawkins is a significant figure, reject faith not just because of their perception of a lack of evidence, but also because of the violence that has been done in the name of religion. The arguments concerning evidence have been addressed for decades, but the rejection of God as homophobic, genocidal and an ethnic cleanser has received far less attention.

A friend who is an engineer shared his concerns that his work on aeroplane landing gear would be used both for commercial airlines and also for military aircraft. My arguments in the previous chapters have explained why I believe in a God of love, revealed in Jesus. But do the same arguments provide a foundation for homophobia and ethnic cleansing?

The easy answer is simply to ignore the parts of the Old Testament that we don't agree with. If it wasn't for my faith that would be fine. But fundamental to a belief in God has to be the humility that we might be wrong, and to look to God's revelation for our authority. In my four sources for theology I gave primacy to God's revelation. But we need our experience and reason, and the cumulative experience and reason of others, to try to discern what God's revelation is.

Jesus used the Old Testament; the New Testament writers frequently quoted the Old Testament. As I said above, 2 Timothy 3:16 states that all the Old Testament is inspired by God.

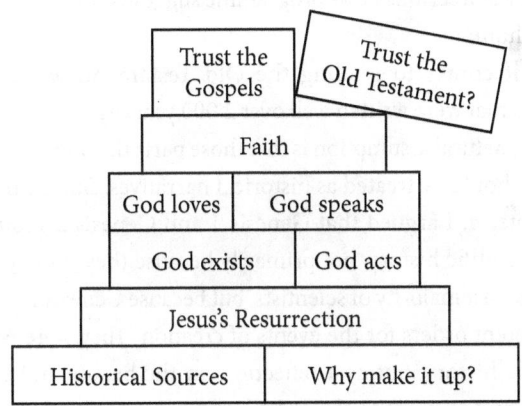

So what do we do with the Old Testament?

What type of documents are they?

When I consider buying a car, there are different sources I might look at. The most accessible are adverts, but I generally ignore them as we know they are written by people who want me to buy the car. As an engineer, I tend to look for technical specifications, and in particular how much it costs, how many miles per gallon it will do, and what size it is—I don't fit well in some small cars. I look for independent reviews, and surveys on how reliable manufacturers have been in the past. Each type of source is different, and we think we know how to interpret them. But are the reviews really independent?

Similarly, when we watch our televisions, we normally know what type of programme we are watching, and therefore how to interpret them. We know that *EastEnders* is a soap opera, and so it is not an accurate depiction of London. We know that *Midsomer Murders* does not reflect our chances of being killed in rural England. We know that *The Vicar of Dibley* and *Rev* do not portray life in ordinary churches, though they might be closer to the truth than you realize! The shows are there for entertainment. Wonderful confusion occurred when *Panorama* produced an April fool report on a failed spaghetti harvest. The audience's preconception that *Panorama* was a serious news programme suggested that it couldn't have a sense of humour.

When it comes to reading the Old Testament, we are reading documents that were written well over 2,000 years ago in a very different culture. My natural assumption is that those parts that look like historical narratives should be treated as historical narratives. But are they?

In chapter 4, I argued that Genesis 1 and Genesis 2 should not be taken as scientific history, not primarily because they disagree with the views of the vast majority of scientists, but because Genesis 1 and Genesis 2 give different orders for the events of creation. They were not written as scientific history, but as a reflection on the beauty and wonder of our world, and to point to the order and purpose behind it. They are a different kind of text with different properties.

Looking at the Old Testament it is obvious that it contains different types of literature. However, it is not certain how we are to interpret them.

Top Gear has won awards for being the best fact-based TV programme. The former presenter, Jeremy Clarkson, was described as a motoring journalist. And yet the programme and Jeremy's writings are full of the most extraordinary exaggeration. For example:

> The Volkswagen Beetle could kill a rain forest at 400 paces whereas today's Golf trundles around with tulips coming out of

its exhaust. The gas coming out of a Saab is actually cleaner than the air that went in. That's true, that is.[48]

This is not true, in the way normal people use the word truth, but he is using exaggeration to make a point. Because we are familiar with the genre, we know how to interpret it.

Exaggeration in the Old Testament historical narratives?

Some readers may have found my allusion to Jeremy Clarkson surprising in a book on theology. However, reading the Old Testament reveals similar exaggeration. In the book of Judges:

> [W]henever the Israelites put in seed, the Midianites and the Amalekites and the people of the east would come up against them. They would encamp against them and destroy the produce of the land, as far as the neighbourhood of Gaza, and leave no sustenance in Israel, and no sheep or ox or donkey.
>
> *Judges 6:3, 4*

If the Midianites literally left no sustenance for Israel, how did the Israelites survive, and where did Gideon get wheat to thresh and the goat and bull he sacrificed further on in the chapter? In the following chapter we read:

> The Midianites and the Amalekites and all the people of the east lay along the valley as thick as locusts; and their camels were without number, countless as the sand on the seashore.
>
> *Judges 7:12*

Camels might be hard to count, but they cannot be without number or literally equivalent to the billions of grains of sand that would make up the smallest beach.

Is this argument for exaggeration a reason to water down some of the most violent parts of the Old Testament?

Concerning the apparent instruction in Deuteronomy 7 to utterly destroy the Hittites and other conquered nations, Moberly's response included pointing out that the phrase "you must utterly destroy them" seems incompatible with the words that follow immediately after:

> Make no covenant with them and show them no mercy. Do not intermarry with them, giving your daughters to their sons or taking their daughters for your sons, for that would turn away your children from following me, to serve other gods.
>
> Deuteronomy 7:2–4

If they were to be utterly destroyed, then there would be no risk of intermarriage. Moberly suggests that "utterly destroy" cannot be the right translation in this context of the underlying Hebrew word "*herem*". He suggests that instead it is a strict command to have nothing to do with them.[49]

The book of Joshua follows Deuteronomy in the Old Testament and appears to show the consequences of the Israelites obeying or failing to obey God's commands in Deuteronomy. However, in the fall of Jericho, the prostitute Rahab is saved, because she helped Israelite spies. According to a literal interpretation of Deuteronomy, Rahab should have been killed as she was a Canaanite. There are no exemptions specified in Deuteronomy. Clearly a literal interpretation does not fit the whole text.

Testimony and counter testimony

However, even with arguments that the commands to genocidal violence can be seen as exaggeration, they still leave me horrified. They also seem incompatible with God's commands depicted elsewhere in the Old Testament. In Deuteronomy, the book that contains the command to utterly destroy the conquered nations, we can also read:

> For the Lord your God is God of gods and Lord of lords, . . . who is not partial and takes no bribe, who executes justice for the orphan and the widow, and who loves the strangers, providing

them with food and clothing. You shall also love the stranger, for you were strangers in the land of Egypt.

Deuteronomy 10:17–19

And in Isaiah 58, God criticizes the Israelites for their superficial worship, while ignoring justice:

Is not this the fast that I choose:
to loose the bonds of injustice, to undo the thongs of the yoke,
to let the oppressed go free, and to break every yoke?
Is it not to share your bread with the hungry,
and bring the homeless poor into your house . . .

Isaiah 58:6, 7

Walter Brueggemann describes these apparent contrasts in the Old Testament as "core testimony and counter testimony".[50] The core testimony speaks of God as shepherd, judge, warrior, provider, father, mother, potter and gardener. It is centred on the account of God saving the people of Israel from slavery, and of his forgiveness and patience when the Israelites fail to trust and obey him. The core testimony does contain numerous warnings of judgement and punishment, indicating that God is concerned with justice, but these are balanced by references to God relenting from punishment and forgiving. The core testimony includes teaching that is a natural consequence of that positive image of God:

If you will only obey the Lord your God, . . . the Lord your God will set you high above all the nations of the earth; all these blessings shall come upon you and overtake you, if you obey the Lord your God.

Deuteronomy 28:1, 2

The Lord is my shepherd, I shall not want.

Psalm 23:1

But the counter testimony reflects the Israelites' experiences that do not seem to fit with this core testimony:

> How long, O Lord? Will you forget me for ever?
> How long will you hide your face from me?
> How long must I bear pain in my soul, and
> have sorrow in my heart all day long?
> How long shall my enemy be exalted over me?
>
> *Psalm 13:1, 2*

> My God, my God, why have you forsaken me?
> Why are you so far from helping me, from
> the words of my groaning?
>
> *Psalm 22:1*

The books of Job and Ecclesiastes wrestle with these questions.

The core testimony led the Israelites to expect blessings following obedience to God. Their counter testimony was that their experience did not always fit with that expectation.

As such I find the Old Testament reflects the struggles I have with God. I am certain that Jesus died on the cross and rose again, and so I am convinced that God exists and loves the world. That is my core testimony. But I have had to take funerals for children and young adults. I have prayed for wars to end only to read news of ongoing torture and violence. The Old Testament speaks of God rescuing Israel from slavery, providing for her in the desert and forgiving her whenever she turned back to him. But it also asks why the good suffer.

Brueggemann opened my eyes to see the testimony and counter testimony. I now see that it doesn't just apply to questions of suffering.

Testimony and counter testimony in God's commands

The description of testimony and counter testimony also fits some surprising aspects of the Old Testament. Deuteronomy 12 states that the Israelites should only offer sacrifices in one place:

> Take care that you do not offer your burnt offerings at any place you happen to see. But only at the place that the Lord will choose in one of your tribes.
>
> *Deuteronomy 12:13*

The chosen place for burnt offerings before the temple was built was the tabernacle.

But in 2 Samuel, David sacrifices in different places, apparently at God's command:

> That day Gad came to David and said to him, 'Go up and erect an altar to the Lord on the threshing-floor of Araunah the Jebusite'. Following Gad's instructions, David went up, as the Lord had commanded.
>
> *2 Samuel 24:18, 19*

Or according to Numbers, only the descendants of Aaron could be priests, and it was only the priests who could offer sacrifices to God:

> The Lord spoke to Aaron: I have given you charge of the offerings made to me, all the holy gifts of the Israelites; I have given them to you and your sons as a priestly portion due to you in perpetuity.
>
> *Numbers 18:8*

But Samuel, who was from the tribe of Judah, offered sacrifices:

> So Samuel took a sucking lamb and offered it as a whole burnt offering to the Lord; Samuel cried out to the Lord for Israel, and the Lord answered him.
>
> *1 Samuel 7:9*

My preconception was that when I read in the Old Testament a command of God, I should not question it. But as the Old Testament has conflicting commands, surely that gives us permission to question?

Did God really say . . . ?

In suggesting that we might question an apparent command of God, words from Genesis 3 are a serious warning:

> Now the serpent was more crafty than any other wild animal that the Lord God had made. He said to the woman, 'Did God say, "You shall not eat from any tree in the garden"?'
>
> *Genesis 3:1*

For readers of a more liberal background than me, it is this verse in particular that makes me hesitate before simply ignoring the genocidal commands, and I hope you can see the reason. Genesis 3 depicts the snake, or the Devil, tempting Adam and Eve to doubt what God had said. I do not believe Genesis 3 is a literal account of how humankind first sinned. Instead it is a vivid description and warning of how we are led astray every day.

For example, according to Matthew's Gospel, Jesus said:

> Love your enemies and pray for those who persecute you . . .
>
> *Matthew 5:44*

But tragically, the Church has at times ignored or watered down Jesus' teaching. By suggesting that we could question God's commands in the Old Testament, am I doing the devil's work?

However, Paul wrote:

> Do not despise the words of prophets, but test everything; hold fast to what is good; abstain from every form of evil.
>
> *1 Thessalonians 5:20*

In Genesis 3, Adam and Eve are depicted as having had the command straight from God. There should have been no reason for doubt. Given the historical analysis of previous chapters, I do not believe we have any reason to doubt that Jesus gave the above command to love. In contrast the apparent contradictions in the Old Testament, the core testimony and counter testimony, seem to give us permission to question. Indeed, that questioning seems to be inherent in the Old Testament. Trusting that the Old Testament is inspired by God suggests that questioning, with appropriate humility, is good.

Walter Brueggemann states:

> The tension between the core testimony and the counter testimony is acute and ongoing. It is my judgement that this tension between the two belongs to the very character and substance of Old Testament Faith, a tension that precludes and resists resolution.[51]

Going back to the TV programme analogy, some of the Old Testament reminds me of BBC's *Question Time*: Questions are asked by the audience to a diverse panel. The answers given are usually contradictory. The BBC leaves it to the viewers to make up their own minds.

Or when it comes to reviews of cars, comparing contradictory reviews is a good way of discerning what issues there might be about a car.

Did God really . . . ?
Earlier I quoted Dawkins' statement that

> The God of the Old Testament is arguably the most unpleasant character in all fiction: jealous and proud of it; a petty, unjust, unforgiving control-freak.

A passage that reflects that character is from 2 Samuel, when David is bringing the Ark of the Covenant to Jerusalem.

> When they came to the threshing-floor of Nacon, Uzzah reached out his hand to the ark of God and took hold of it, for the oxen shook it. The anger of the Lord was kindled against Uzzah; and God struck him there because he reached out his hand to the ark; and he died there beside the ark of God.
>
> *2 Samuel 6:6, 7*

So Uzzah touched the Ark because he was concerned for it, and as a result was killed. And yet in Exodus 34, when God passes before Moses, he declares his name:

> The Lord, the Lord, a God merciful and gracious, slow to anger, and abounding in steadfast love and faithfulness . . .
>
> *Exodus 34:6*

The phrase "slow to anger" occurs twelve times in the Old Testament in descriptions of God. It is part of the core testimony. But the account of Uzzah being killed paints a different picture.

Christian teaching frequently reflects only the core testimony, depicting God as shepherd, saviour and provider, slow to anger and abounding in steadfast love. In contrast Dawkins' quote reflects the counter testimony, portraying a God who appears vindictive and violent.

Following Brueggemann's argument, my understanding is that we can only begin to understand the depth of the Old Testament when we hold the two sides in tension. The Old Testament reflects the real arguments and discussion of the Jewish people as they wrestled with their theology. Did God really kill Uzzah for touching the Ark?

When it comes to questions of why God allows suffering, then those questions are just as relevant today. Acknowledging that tension should guard us from making statements that reflect only one side of the Old Testament. The tension also gives me glimpses of God who does not fit my preconceptions.

The statement from 2 Timothy 3:16 that "[a]ll scripture is inspired by God and is useful for teaching, for reproof, for correction, and for training in righteousness" does not mean that scripture is without error. It doesn't mean that it has all the answers. Rather: it is *useful*. Thinking about my four sources for theology, the Old Testament is a mixture of their understanding of God's revelation, their experience and their reason.

As an engineer, some things we can know for certain. Other areas are much more open to question. My faith in Jesus' death and resurrection I consider certain. The tensions inherent in the Old Testament fit into the uncertain category. We may never know the answers, but those answers are not crucial for my faith. I will keep asking the questions.

Thoughts of asking questions also speaks of a complementary way of looking at the Old Testament. Talking about testimony and counter testimony alone might suggest that the Old Testament just leaves us stuck in the mud. But reading all of the Old Testament also suggests a journey and a progression of thought, an adventure.

The Old Testament as journey

In Psalm 137:7 we read:

> O daughter Babylon, you devastator!
> Happy shall they be who pay you back
>   what you have done to us!
> Happy shall they be who take your little ones
>   and dash them against the rock!

The word translated here as "happy" is elsewhere translated as "blessed". How can we describe this scripture as "God-breathed" when it appears to be encouraging the violent killing of babies?

But, of course, this is a psalm, a prayer. The psalm was written as a lament when the Israelites were in exile in Babylon and reflects the anger and bitterness they felt. It encourages us to take our anger and bitterness to God in prayer. It doesn't mean that God agrees with our proposals.

William Webb, in his book *Slaves, Women & Homosexuals: Exploring the Hermeneutics of Cultural Analysis*, writes about how the culture of the time influenced the text. The text in some ways reflects the culture of the time, and God's response to that culture:

> The way that the Bible deals with slaves, as well as numerous other topics, should convince us of the influence of culture on the formation of the text. Scripture does not present a "finalized ethic" in every area of human relationship. God challenges his covenant people to act redemptively in the area of slavery (e.g.,

release for Hebrew slaves every seventh year, provisions upon release, limitations on beatings, slave-free equality statements). The text takes us on a journey that clearly involves restoration of the society to which the text was given. However, to stop where the Bible stops (with its isolated words) ultimately fails to reapply the redemptive spirit of the text as it spoke to the original audience. It fails to see that further reformation is possible and that further reformation must happen in order to fulfil the spirit-based component of meaning within the text's words.[52]

For example, the Old Testament commands concerning slavery were radical for their time. They gave slaves some rights:

> When a slave-owner strikes a male or female slave with a rod and the slave dies immediately, the owner shall be punished. But if the slave survives for a day or two, there is no punishment; for the slave is the owner's property.
>
> When a slave-owner strikes the eye of a male or female slave, destroying it, the owner shall let the slave go, a free person, to compensate for the eye. If the owner knocks out a tooth of a male or female slave, the slave shall be let go, a free person, to compensate for the tooth.
>
> Exodus 21:20,21,26,27

However, we should not conclude that this Old Testament form of slavery is good. It was just a step in the right direction.

Webb makes similar arguments for the Old Testament treatment of women. For example:

> When a man sells his daughter as a slave, she shall not go out as the male slaves do. If she does not please her master, who designated her for himself, then he shall let her be redeemed; he shall have no right to sell her to a foreign people, since he has dealt unfairly with her. If he designates her for his son, he shall deal with her as with a daughter. If he takes another wife to himself, he shall not diminish the food, clothing, or marital

rights of the first wife. And if he does not do these three things for her, she shall go out without debt, without payment of money.

Exodus 21:7–11

To our ears this way of treating women as property is an awful form of abuse, but Webb argues that it was a significant step forward in that culture.

Webb argues that the "texts of terror" concerning women and slaves do not reflect God's will per se, but point to a process of change. They are not a finalized ethic, but a step on the way. This of course leaves questions of "why didn't God enforce his final ethic back then?" A question which goes along with the unanswered questions of suffering.

If we can apply this argument to ameliorate the shock of the Old Testament's treatment of women and slaves, can we also look at the violence of the Old Testament in a different way? Please note that I am asking questions, and from the Old Testament alone; I am very unsure of the answers.

The Old Testament as treasure—salvation history

This chapter has been difficult to write, because I have questions, not answers. When I read the "texts of terror", I feel uncomfortable, but they are only a fraction of the Old Testament. The Old Testament as a whole is an extraordinary story. It starts with accounts of God's creation and that we were created to care for it and to have a relationship with God. But we made a mess of it. Those early chapters speak not just of events in the past but of problems today. The Old Testament then recounts stories of God's call to individuals to begin a journey of salvation. I love the stories of Abraham, Jacob, Joseph, and Moses that speak of their failings and God changing them. They speak of God being faithful to his promises, rescuing the Jews from slavery, and giving them laws including the Ten Commandments. They speak of the Jews' failure to obey, and God's faithfulness and forbearance, and also of his anger at injustice. They speak of the Old Covenant, whereby if only the Jews would obey, God would bless. The Old Covenant failed, because it did not lead to obedience, or to God's kingdom in its fullness, but it was not the end of the story, it was just the first part of the journey.

My faith is not built on the Old Testament. It is built on my understanding of Jesus' life, death and resurrection. The Old Testament provides the context for Jesus' ministry. He was a Jew, who read and knew the Old Testament. The Old Testament spoke of the future, when God would send his Messiah, when God's salvation would come.

Hebrews 1:1–3 states:

> Long ago God spoke to our ancestors in many and various ways by the prophets, but in these last days he has spoken to us by a Son, whom he appointed heir of all things, through whom he also created the worlds. He is the reflection of God's glory and the exact imprint of God's very being.

The Old Testament may hint at the answers to our questions, but it can be interpreted in very different ways. It is not God's final word, but only the first part of the story. Concerning the texts of terror, I am left with questions, but with Jesus I find some answers. In particular, Jesus reveals what God is like. And so it is to Jesus that I turn again in the next chapter.

CHAPTER 7

So Who Was Jesus?

In engineering I specialized in metal fatigue in railway lines. Normal metal fatigue cracks grow when the faces of the crack separate under load. Each separation causes a small increase in the crack length. This is known as Mode I fatigue. The cracks I studied were a mystery. All the analysis of the rolling contact stresses between the wheel and the rail revealed that the crack faces slid over one another, a shearing motion rather than an opening motion. Cracks had been shown to grow by shearing—Mode II fatigue—but only for a maximum of about a millimetre before the crack would change direction to become a Mode I crack. But these cracks in rails could grow for 25mm or more. My predecessor on the project had noted research which showed that these cracks didn't grow in dry conditions. Adding water to the stress analysis model predicted that water trapped in the crack could give a Mode I opening just before the larger Mode II shearing movement. In my research I replicated this sequential Mode I and Mode II fatigue cycle and to our delight the cracks grew straight, without branching. The mystery was solved.[53]

I write this partly because I thought you might be interested in my research, but more relevantly because the journey of discovery has some parallels for me with my own journey considering the mystery of who Jesus is. Traditional Christian teaching holds that Jesus is both God and man, but how can you have a composite God—Man? What is the evidence? How did the Church, and how did I, come to our conclusions? Like my research, the Church's understanding developed with time.

The Myth of God Incarnate?

When I was a teenager, one book that sent shockwaves through the Church was *The Myth of God Incarnate,* edited by John Hick.[54] The heart of the book was the belief that Jesus was not God Incarnate—God in human form—but that Jesus was simply a man. According to the authors he was a good man, a teacher, a prophet, but not God. It is a view that was popular in the 1970s and probably reflects what many believe about Jesus today.

Behind the title was another question, as to whether all world faiths could be made compatible. It was in part, I think, a reaction to the arrogance of the Western/Christian world, believing that we must be right, and everyone else wrong. If Jesus was simply a good man, then the divisions between the world faiths would be much less. Islam, for example, accepts Jesus as a prophet.

Though I don't agree with the conclusions of *The Myth of God Incarnate,* I do think that it is healthy for us to pause and consider what we believe and why we believe it, rather than just accepting unquestioningly what we have been taught. To declare that I am right and others are wrong, without considering why they disagree, is not just arrogant but stupid.

The next crucial question for my faith is: Who was Jesus?

The search for the historical Jesus

When I was at university in Durham, I discovered that in the academic world this question was addressed in what was known as the "search for the historical Jesus". In Burkett's summary of this, his conclusion is largely negative. He wrote that those involved in the research considered that the only significant sources for the life of Jesus were the Gospels and that they did not trust them. The problem was: "How could they distinguish the authentic tradition in the Gospels from traditions that originated in the Church?"[55]

My reaction to reading this is to ask why those involved in the quest were so convinced that the Early Church would make things up? And given that the Church started its growth and teaching within weeks of

Jesus' death, if they were teaching a pack of lies why did anyone believe them?

Burkett comments that the conclusions of the search for the historical Jesus portray a purely human Jesus. He states that they arrived at this conclusion because of the assumptions held by the interpreters:

1. That theological claims about God's activity in the world fall outside the realm of history, which deals only with the human world.
2. That the theological and supernatural claims of the Gospels do not pass the criteria of authenticity.
3. That supernatural events do not happen.[56]

I find this frustrating. The Church persecuted Copernicus and Galileo for saying that the earth and the other planets went round the sun. The Church did so because of their presuppositions about the universe, rather than looking at the evidence. It seems pointless to do research concerning Jesus' divinity based on assumptions that the supernatural does not exist.

However, in spite of my frustrations, I still find the summary of the quest for the historical Jesus helpful. The editors of *The Historical Jesus in Context* write:

> Most scholars agree that Jesus:
> - was baptized by John
> - debated with fellow Jews on how best to live according to God's will
> - engaged in healings and exorcisms
> - taught in parables
> - gathered male and female followers in Galilee, went to Jerusalem, and was crucified by Roman soldiers during the governorship of Pontius Pilate.[57]

We were taught that the researchers felt that the search for the historical Jesus was a failure, but for me those five points seem a pretty good summary of Jesus' life.

Was Jesus more than a prophet?

In contrast to the presuppositions listed by Burkett, I started this book by questioning my assumptions as to whether God exists and whether the miraculous might happen. My conclusion, that God does exist, was based on the evidence for Jesus' resurrection.

My next logical question is whether Jesus is God. In the Gospels there are others who are said to have been raised from the dead and there are no claims that they were anything other than human. Relevant to this is the question from chapter 5 of whether the claims made by Jesus about himself in John's Gospel are compatible with the picture portrayed by Matthew, Mark and Luke.

Here is my argument for why I believe that Jesus is God, rather than just a prophet, based on the Gospels of Matthew, Mark and Luke. It is an argument that you could find in similar form in many "Christian basics" courses today.

Consider the following passages from Luke's Gospel:

> When he came to Nazareth, ... [h]e stood up to read: ... 'The Spirit of the Lord is upon me, because he has anointed me to bring good news to the poor. He has sent me to proclaim release to the captives and recovery of sight to the blind, to let the oppressed go free, to proclaim the year of the Lord's favour.' And he rolled up the scroll, ... Then he began to say to them, 'Today this scripture has been fulfilled in your hearing.'
>
> *Luke 4:16–21*

> Everyone then who hears these words of mine and acts on them will be like a wise man who built his house on rock. The rain fell, the floods came, and the winds blew and beat on that house, but it did not fall, because it had been founded on rock.
>
> *Matthew 7:24–25*

> You have heard that it was said, "An eye for an eye and a tooth for a tooth." But I say to you, Do not resist an evildoer. But if anyone strikes you on the right cheek, turn the other also . . .
>
> Matthew 5:38–39

Imagine someone coming to a church today and saying that things written in the Bible hundreds of years ago were written about them. My first reaction would be that they were either mad or dangerously manipulative.

If they then said that their words were so wonderful that a life built on them would cope with any storm, I wouldn't believe them.

Or imagine someone saying in a church, "Jesus said . . . but I say to you . . . " The Jews hearing Jesus say this 2,000 years ago would have known that it was Moses who had said: "an eye for an eye and a tooth for a tooth." And Moses had had the commands directly from God at Mount Sinai. They were part of the founding constitution of the people of Israel. The Jews thought they were special because they were the only nation on earth that God had chosen as his people. The laws from Moses symbolized that unique relationship with the creator of the heavens and the earth. And yet Jesus essentially was saying, "Forget what Moses said. Listen to me." Jesus wasn't saying that he was a prophet and that he had a message from God. He was saying: "Listen to ME!"

C. S. Lewis, the author of the Narnia stories, used these passages to argue for Jesus's divinity in what has come to be described as the mad, bad or God "trilemma". The claims that Jesus made explicitly or implicitly in the above passages give us a choice. Jesus was either mad, in the sense that he believed the claims about himself as some people might believe they are Napoleon Bonaparte. Or he was deliberately lying, and so dangerously manipulative. Or he was and is the Son of God. He left no space for us consider him to be just a good, moral teacher. And of course, those who are seriously deluded don't inspire people in the way Jesus did. Jesus had no reason to deliberately lie – he didn't gain anything from it. If he was intent on gaining power he could have led an armed rebellion. Instead, his claims led him to be killed on the cross.[58]

Personally, I am convinced by Lewis' argument. I trust the Gospels as a summary of Jesus' public teachings and actions and from that conclude that he must have been more than a prophet. But it is still a significant step from there to the Christian claim that Jesus is God incarnate, God made flesh, and that God is Trinity: Father, Son and Holy Spirit.

Is Jesus God?

As a teenager, I worked through these arguments, so that I was convinced that Jesus rose from the dead and that he was more than a prophet. However, if you had asked me why I believed that Jesus was God, I would have struggled to give a good answer. I would have thought that the Bible simply said so, but I would not have known where. I now know that the answer is more complicated.

When I was in Durham, we had seminars based on our Professor James Dunn's book *Unity and Diversity in the New Testament*.[59] One of the questions he posed was whether there was diversity of opinion in the New Testament about whether or not Jesus was God.

In other lectures and through reading I discovered that the great ecumenical councils of the Early Church debated the nature of Jesus in great detail, and that it was an issue that divided the Early Church from the second century onwards.

I do now believe that Jesus was and is God, and that God is Father, Son and Holy Spirit: three in one. But the route to getting there took some time. My eventual answer to Professor Dunn's question was that the New Testament shows that the Early Church took time to come to understand that Jesus was God, and that Jesus himself did not state it explicitly.

Titles for Jesus in Matthew, Mark and Luke

In the first three Gospels, Jesus' normal way of referring to himself is as the Son of Man. In the Jewish context this would probably have been seen as a claim to be the "Messiah", God's special anointed leader, referred to by prophecies in the book of Daniel (Daniel 7:13,14). Elsewhere in Matthew, Mark and Luke, Jesus is described as God's Son:

At his baptism a voice came from heaven and declared, "This is my son, the Beloved, with whom I am well pleased." (Matthew 3:17, also in Mark 1:11 and Luke 3:22).

The devil in his temptation asks, "If you are the Son of God . . . " (Matthew 4:1–11, Luke 4:1–13).

In his transfiguration the voice again comes from heaven: "This is my Son, the Beloved; listen to him." (Mark 9:7).

Jesus also refers to God as "my Father" forty-one times, starting when he was in the temple as a child (Luke 2:49).

According to Matthew, Peter then puts this together, claiming that Jesus is more than a prophet: "You are the Messiah, the Son of the living God." (Matthew 16:16).

Matthew, Mark and Luke all explicitly refer to Jesus as the Messiah and Son of God. However, Jesus also instructed his disciples to call God their Father in the Lord's Prayer, presumably indicating that they too could consider themselves children of God (Matthew 6:9, Luke 11:2). It is also quite a step from Son of God to God.

Titles for Jesus in John's Gospel

In John's Gospel, Jesus claims to be

- the bread of life (John 6:35)

- the light of the world (John 8:12)

- the gate to salvation (John 10:9)

- the good shepherd (John 10:11)

- the resurrection and the life (John 11:25)

the way, the truth and the life (John 14:6)

the true vine (John 15:1).

And in John 8:58, Jesus said, "Very truly, I tell you, before Abraham was, I am." Then, in John 14:9–10,18–20, Jesus says:

> Whoever has seen me has seen the Father. How can you say "Show us the Father"? Do you not believe that I am in the Father and the Father is in me?
> I will not leave you orphaned; I am coming to you. In a little while the world will no longer see me, but you will see me; because I live, you also will live. On that day you will know that I am in my Father, and you in me, and I in you.

As in the first three Gospels, the above texts affirm Jesus as more than a prophet. He is in the Father and the Father is in him. But as he also said that the disciples could be in him, saying that he is in the Father is not the same as explicitly saying he is God.

It is only in the opening verses of John's Gospel that we have more unambiguous teaching that Jesus is God. These words were written by the Gospel author, not said specifically by Jesus himself:

> In the beginning was the Word, and the Word was with God, and the Word was God. He was in the beginning with God. All things came into being through him, and without him not one thing came into being. What has come into being in him was life, and the life was the light of all people. The light shines in the darkness, and the darkness did not overcome it.
> He was in the world, and the world came into being through him; yet the world did not know him. He came to what was his own, and his own people did not accept him. But to all who received him, who believed in his name, he gave power to become children of God, who were born, not of blood or of the will of the flesh or of the will of man, but of God.

> And the Word became flesh and lived among us, and we have seen his glory, the glory as of a father's only son, full of grace and truth.
>
> *John 1:1–5,10–14*

And then, when Thomas encounters Jesus after his resurrection:

> Jesus came and stood among them and said, 'Peace be with you.' Then he said to Thomas, 'Put your finger here and see my hands. Reach out your hand and put it in my side. Do not doubt but believe.' Thomas answered him, 'My Lord and my God!'
>
> *John 20:26–28*

It is odd, to put it mildly, that Jesus makes no unequivocal statement that he is God, and yet it is so explicitly stated in our creeds.

In Durham I learned a partial answer to this conundrum. It is known as the "Messianic secret". The logic behind this is that if Jesus had declared to the Jews that he was God, their shock and outrage would have been so great that he would not have been able to carry out his mission. His more overt statements, as we find them in chapters 14 to 16 of John's Gospel, were private conversations with his disciples shortly before his arrest and crucifixion. Even in them he declares that he has more to tell them than they can bear and that they need to wait for the Holy Spirit to lead them into all truth (John 16:12, 13).

Titles for Jesus in Acts and the Epistles.

In many of Paul's letters he opens with the greeting:

> Grace to you and peace from God our Father and the Lord Jesus Christ.
>
> *Romans 1:7; cf. 1 Corinthians 1:3*

In his speech to the Jews on the day of Pentecost, Peter says:

> Therefore let the entire house of Israel know with certainty that God has made him both Lord and Messiah, this Jesus whom you crucified.
>
> *Acts 2:36*

In some passages we have more detailed descriptions of their understanding of the nature of Jesus. In the letter to the Colossians we read:

> He is the image of the invisible God, the firstborn of all creation; for in him all things in heaven and on earth were created, things visible and invisible, whether thrones or dominions or rulers or powers—all things have been created through him and for him. He himself is before all things, and in him all things hold together. He is the head of the body, the church; he is the beginning, the firstborn from the dead, so that he might come to have first place in everything. For in him all the fullness of God was pleased to dwell . . .
>
> *Colossians 1:15-19*

And in Philippians Paul writes that Jesus

> though he was in the form of God, did not regard equality with God as something to be exploited, but emptied himself, taking the form of a slave, being born in human likeness. And being found in human form, he humbled himself and became obedient to the point of death—even death on a cross. Therefore God also highly exalted him and gave him the name that is above every name, so that at the name of Jesus every knee should bend, in heaven and on earth and under the earth, and every tongue should confess that Jesus Christ is Lord, to the glory of God the Father.
>
> *Philippians 2:6-11*

In the letter to the Hebrews the unknown author writes:

> Long ago God spoke to our ancestors in many and various ways by the prophets, but in these last days he has spoken to us by a Son, whom he appointed heir of all things, through whom he also created the worlds. He is the reflection of God's glory and the exact imprint of God's very being, and he sustains all things by his powerful word. When he had made purification for sins, he sat down at the right hand of the Majesty on high, having become as much superior to angels as the name he has inherited is more excellent than theirs.
>
> *Hebrews 1:1-4*

From my reading of the New Testament, as well as at the beginning of John's Gospel, and Thomas' statement after his resurrection, Jesus is described as the Son of God, the exact image or reflection of God, in whom the fullness of God dwelt, and through whom all things were created. That description clearly states that Jesus is far more than a prophet, but to my mind falls short of the formula used by the Nicene Creed:

> God from God, Light from Light, true God from true God, begotten, not made, of one Being with the Father.

The development of theology in the Early Church

From the lectures and my reading when I was at Durham, and reading Alister McGrath's *Introduction to Christian Theology* more recently, I understand that the Creed, as we have it now, developed from the second century onwards, especially in response to the "Arian controversy".[60] We do not have any of the original writings of Arius, so our knowledge is based on the writings of Athanasius in his arguments against Arianism. Athanasius stated that Arius wrote:

> "God was not always a Father;" but "once God was alone, and not yet a Father, but afterwards He became a Father." "The Son was not always;" for, whereas all things were made out of nothing,

and all existing creatures and works were made, so the Word of God Himself was "made out of nothing," and "once He was not," and "He was not before His origination," but He as others "had an origin of creation."[61]

I have tried reading a translation of Athanasius' writing, but I don't recommend it! According to McGrath's summary,[62] Athanasius' argument was primarily based on John's Gospel, and his insistence that the title Son of God was not to be interpreted metaphorically, or as an honorific title.

Athanasius also stressed that the Church prayed to Jesus and worshipped him. If Jesus was a creature—created by the Father—then Christians would be guilty of worshipping a creature. Christians, from the Old Testament, are commanded to worship God and him alone. This demonstrates how important the debate concerning Jesus' divinity is, but it is not a conclusive argument for Jesus' divinity—Christians can get things wrong!

The most significant part of Athanasius' argument was that only God could save. According to Mcgrath, Athanasius argues that because only God can save, and the gospels and epistles describe Jesus as our saviour, then Jesus must be God.[63]

I will return to this in the next chapter.

In the end, Athanasius won the argument, and the Greek behind our Creed says that Jesus is *homoousios* or "of the same substance or being" as the Father, rather than *homoiousios*—"of like substance or like being" to the Father.

The arguments concerning the exact nature of the Trinity, and how Jesus could be both God and man, continued through the ecumenical councils of Ephesus (431 CE) and Chalcedon (451 CE), resulting in the Athanasian Creed which can be found in the Church of England's *Book of Common Prayer*:

> WHOSOEVER will be saved: before all things it is necessary that he hold the Catholick Faith. Which Faith except every one do keep whole and undefiled: without doubt he shall perish everlastingly.
>
> And the Catholick Faith is this:

> That we worship one God in Trinity, and Trinity in Unity; Neither confounding the Persons: nor dividing the Substance.
>
> For there is one Person of the Father, another of the Son: and another of the Holy Ghost.
>
> But the Godhead of the Father, of the Son, and of the Holy Ghost, is all one: the Glory equal, the Majesty co-eternal.
>
> Such as the Father is, such is the Son: and such is the Holy Ghost.
>
> The Father uncreate, the Son uncreate: and the Holy Ghost uncreate.
>
> The Father incomprehensible, the Son incomprehensible: and the Holy Ghost incomprehensible.
>
> The Father eternal, the Son eternal: and the Holy Ghost eternal.
>
> And yet they are not three eternals: but one eternal . . . .
>
> So the Father is God, the Son is God: and the Holy Ghost is God.
>
> And yet they are not three Gods: but one God . . .

My reaction at Durham, and now, is to be uncomfortable with trying to define the nature of God so precisely. I was equally uncomfortable with the vehemence of the attacks on so-called heretics, and the apparent political power struggles behind the later councils.[64]

The Creed gives us a formula of God being both three and one which is mathematically impossible. I am happy with that formula in that it speaks of the mystery of God. As in engineering, some things are beyond our understanding, but we can build with what we know. In my personal theology, I am happy for the nature of God to be a mystery.

What disturbs me from the Athanasian Creed, however, is the statement that:

> WHOSOEVER will be saved: before all things it is necessary that he hold the Catholick Faith. Which Faith except every one do keep whole and undefiled: without doubt he shall perish everlastingly.

It therefore says that holding this faith is essential to salvation. I wonder how many of my congregation would be able to make sense of the Athanasian Creed. It also disturbs me that all the energy and debate surrounded the "speculative metaphysics", rather than looking at Jesus' death on the cross and its significance for us today.

This brought me back to McGrath's summary of Athanasius's argument, that because only God can save, and the Gospels and epistles describe Jesus as our saviour, then Jesus must be God.

My belief in Jesus being both fully God and fully human, and my belief in the Trinity, now rests on my struggle to understand the significance of Jesus' death on the cross, as I will explain in the next part of this book.

PART 3

Why?

CHAPTER 8

Why Did Jesus Die, and What Does That Say about God?

As an engineer, I am fascinated by how things work. At the National Railway Museum, in York, I loved seeing the insides of a steam train opened up. It showed how the steam was produced, used to provide power, and then condensed, heating more steam in the process. I loved seeing how the engineering I had learnt in lectures was applied in real life decades ago, and I loved the craftsmanship. But what about the cross? How does that work? Why did Jesus have to die? And following on from the last chapter, what does that say about who Jesus is?

As a child, teenager and young adult I remember hearing preachers explaining the significance of Jesus' death on the cross in various ways:

1. A man found himself in court, knowing he was guilty of a crime. To his shock, the judge was his brother/father/old friend. The judge, as a judge, declared him guilty and sentenced him to pay a large fine. Then the judge, as father/brother/friend took off his wig, came down and paid the fine.
2. God made us to have a relationship with him. *The preacher has one hand and fingers pointing upwards, linking with the other hand and fingers pointing downwards.* But we made a mess of that relationship by disobeying God. *Preacher puts a book on top of the lower hand symbolizing a barrier between us and God.* We are helpless. We cannot get through the barrier. So God came down, as Jesus, took the barrier from us and put it on himself, dealt with it, and so restored our relationship with God.

Or my favourite:

3. Graham was a schoolboy who was always being told off. He was not good at being good. He was not good at sitting still or paying attention. He was in the back row of a class. Mr Booth was the rather strict teacher. While Mr Booth's back was turned, Graham chewed gum, which was not allowed. When the chewing gum lost its flavour, Graham decided to flick it at Julie, sitting on the front row. But Graham was not very good at flicking gum. Just as he flicked it, Mr Booth turned. Instead of hitting Julie, the gum hit Mr Booth on the forehead and stuck in his fringe. Mr Booth turned red with anger. He was fairly certain that Graham had flicked the gum, but he did not actually see it. He demanded that someone owned up, but no one said anything. Graham was tired of being told off. Mr Booth declared that the class could not go out to play until someone owned up. The bell rang and they could see the rest of the school going out to the playground. "You cannot go out until someone is willing to take the blame", said Mr Booth. Then to his shock, Jimmy put his hand up. Mr Booth had never known Jimmy to be naughty. He sent the class out and then asked Jimmy if he really flicked the gum. Jimmy, who would not lie, said no. "So why did you put your hand up?" "I didn't put my hand up when you asked who did it, because I didn't flick the gum. But then you said no one could go out to play until someone was willing to take the blame. I am willing to take the blame."

All the above have their roots in biblical explanations:

Jesus' death as a sacrifice, payment or ransom

The most frequent explanation for Jesus' death uses the language of sacrifice. The Old Testament gave instructions that the Jews should sacrifice animals to obtain forgiveness for their sins, where sin is defined as any transgression of the God-given laws (e.g. Leviticus 4 and 5). In addition, on the Day of Atonement, as well as sacrificing sin offerings, a scapegoat was ceremonially sent into the desert, bearing the sins of the people (Leviticus 16:3–22).

In John's Gospel, John the Baptist declared when he saw Jesus:

> "Here is the Lamb of God who takes away the sin of the world!"
> *John 1:29*

At the Last Supper, the final meal Jesus ate with his disciples before he died, Jesus took the cup of wine and said:

> [F]or this is my blood of the covenant, which is poured out for many for the forgiveness of sins.
> *Matthew 26:28*

Paul wrote:

> For there is no distinction, since all have sinned and fall short of the glory of God; they are now justified by his grace as a gift, through the redemption that is in Christ Jesus, whom God put forward as a sacrifice of atonement by his blood, effective through faith.
> *Romans 3:22–25*

In the above quotation, Paul also writes that the sacrifice brought about our redemption. In New Testament times, someone who got into a debt that they could not pay could be sold as a slave. Their only hope of being set free would be if someone else, a family member or friend, would come and pay the price, and redeem them. We still use the word redemption today in the context of a pawnbroker's, where someone might leave a wedding ring in return for money. The only way to redeem the ring would be to pay back the money and the interest. So Paul wrote:

> Christ redeemed us from the curse of the law by becoming a curse for us . . .
> *Galatians 3:13*

In 1 Timothy 2:6, 1 Peter 1:18 and Revelation 5:9 we also have the image of Christ's death being a ransom paid to set us free, as a kidnapper might demand a ransom for the release of their victim:

> You know that you were ransomed from the futile ways inherited from your ancestors, not with perishable things like silver or gold, but with the precious blood of Christ, like that of a lamb without defect or blemish.
>
> 1 Peter 1:18,19

But who is the sacrifice to?

The New Testament writers described Jesus' death as being like a sacrifice, a payment or a ransom, which resulted in us being forgiven and set free from sin. I learnt at Durham that these models have been championed and debated over the centuries. Anselm in particular stuck in my mind. In his treatise entitled *Cur Deus homo* (Why God became man), he argued that because of our sin, satisfaction had to be made. We cannot provide that satisfaction, so God became man to pay it for us. This explanation is often termed "substitutionary atonement".

The trouble with any of these metaphorical explanations is that a payment, ransom or sacrifice has to be paid to someone. Who is that someone? The natural interpretation of the stories is to picture God the Father as the angry judge, teacher or slave owner, who is recompensed or satisfied. God the Father gets his pound of flesh, with Jesus paying the price.

Steve Chalke in his thought-provoking book, *The Lost Message of Jesus*, describes this type of model as "cosmic child abuse".[65] We have sinned and so God the Father wants his Son to pay the price. John Stott, in *The Cross of Christ*, writes that such a simplistic understanding:

> [d]enigrates the Father. Reluctant to suffer himself, he victimises Christ instead. Reluctant to forgive, he is prevailed upon by Christ to do so. He is seen as the pitiless ogre whose wrath has

to be assuaged, whose disinclination to act has to be overcome, by the loving self-sacrifice of Jesus.[66]

But if Jesus was not paying the price to God the Father, what was happening?

My own understanding of the cross was changed when I read Jürgen Moltmann's article "The Crucified God" in *Theology Today*, when I was at Durham. In it Moltmann describes the suffering of God the Father, in the agony of watching his son die:

> Jesus suffers dying in abandonment, but he does not suffer death because death itself is not something one can "suffer". The Father, however, in the pain of his love, suffers the death of his son . . . Because the dying of the Son is something other than the pain of the Father, one cannot speak absolutely of God's death as occurs in the God-is-dead theology. To understand the suffering and the death in God, one must speak in trinitarian terms and must set aside the simple monotheistic concept of God.[67]

The paper transformed my understanding of the cross as a Trinitarian event. In other words, if we think of God as three gods, Father, Son and Holy Spirit, then the cross does appear like "cosmic child abuse": the wrathful Father God demanding the sacrifice; the loving Son of God paying the price on our behalf. But as I changed to see God as one God, suffering as both Father and Son, then the cross was transformed. It was twice the agony, with both the Father and the Son paying the price.

Why I am convinced that Jesus is God

Going back to the last chapter, and the question of why the Church declares Jesus to be God, it is Jesus' death on the cross that convinces me that Jesus is fully God as well as being fully human, and that God is truly Trinitarian. If Jesus was anything less than fully God, how could God allow such a travesty of justice? If God was in some way three gods, how could the Father allow the Son to suffer? But because God is both three and one, then both Father and Son suffer on the cross. I do not pretend that I understand the Trinity, or that it "makes sense" in the way that carbon fibre or an internal combustion engine makes sense to me. The heart of the Trinity, and the event of the cross, will always be a mystery, but a wonderful mystery.

Why was the cross necessary?

However, this does not explain why the cross was necessary. Why couldn't God just forgive us our sins without going through the agony? I have heard it said that the side of God who demands justice needs the sacrifice to be paid. But to my mind it does not sound like justice if someone else is punished for something I did. Many of us long for justice when we see the evil around us in the world, and we would want the people who commit the crimes to pay the penalty.

Stott argues that the sacrifice needs to be paid because of the holy nature of God:

> We must therefore hold fast to the biblical revelation of the living God who hates evil, is disgusted and angered by it, and refuses ever to come to terms with it. In consequence, we may be sure that, when he searched in his mercy for some way to forgive, cleanse and accept evil doers, it was not along the road of moral compromise. It had to be a way which was expressive equally of his love and of his wrath.[68]

He backs up this argument with R. W. Dale's words in his book *Atonement*:

> It is partly because sin does not provoke our own wrath, that we do not believe it provokes the wrath of God.[69]

I agree that there are grave theological dangers in overlooking the horror of sin. Having looked at my own life and my knowledge of the world, I know the need for us to acknowledge the terrible evil around us. But I do not agree that God hates evil so much that he cannot forgive without a price being paid. Looking at the Bible itself, the Old Testament frequently talks of God's forgiveness, and John the Baptist's message was a baptism of repentance for the forgiveness of sins. That forgiveness was not linked directly with the cross. The problem, then, is not that God cannot forgive without Jesus' death on the cross. God is a forgiving God by his nature. The problem is that evil itself cannot be defeated without the cross.

John Stott quotes Habakkuk 1:13, reflecting that it was the opinion of the Old Testament writers that God hated evil so much that he could not bear to have anything to do with it:

> Your eyes are too pure to behold evil, and you cannot look on wrongdoing ...
>
> *Habakkuk 1:13*[70]

However, I think Jesus shows that Habakkuk was wrong. Jesus was frequently seen in the company of so-called sinners:

> When the Pharisees saw this, they said to his disciples, 'Why does your teacher eat with tax-collectors and sinners?' But when he heard this, he said, 'Those who are well have no need of a physician, but those who are sick. Go and learn what this means, "I desire mercy, not sacrifice." For I have come to call not the righteous but sinners.'
>
> *Matthew 9:11–13*

When the scribes and the Pharisees grumbled that Jesus welcomed sinners and ate with them, Jesus responded by telling the parables of the lost sheep, the lost coin and the lost (or prodigal) son. The parables make it clear that all of us are precious in God's sight. They speak of God's love that weeps because of sin and its consequences, rather than God's wrath that cannot bear to be close to sin.

I have had the misfortune to have blocked drains, and sewage seeping up onto my drive as a consequence. The sewage was disgusting, but my desire to get rid of it meant that I lifted the manhole cover and sorted it. I think that speaks to me of God's hatred for sin, and his passion for saving sinners. Of course, unlike me, God did not protect himself by using draining rods and rubber gloves or by calling the professionals when my amateur attempts failed.

By Jesus' death, we can be washed clean
Speaking of drains, a striking image for what Jesus made possible through the cross is that of being washed clean:

> But you were washed, you were sanctified, you were justified in the name of the Lord Jesus Christ and in the Spirit of our God.
> *1 Corinthians 6:11*

> Husbands, love your wives, just as Christ loved the church and gave himself up for her, in order to make her holy by cleansing her with the washing of water by the word, so as to present the church to himself in splendour, without a spot or wrinkle or anything of the kind—yes, so that she may be holy and without blemish.
> *Ephesians 5:25-27*

In our current Church of England liturgy, we are invited to confess our sins shortly after the start of the service, as if we could not come close to God until our sin had been dealt with. But in the Parable of the Prodigal Son, before the son said a word, the father had rushed out to meet him. Before the son could give his full speech of repentance the father called for a robe, sandals and a ring—signs that the son was to be treated as his son. In the Lord's Prayer, Jesus did command that we should pray "forgive us our sins", but it is near the end of the prayer, not at the beginning. It strikes me that we should never think that God cannot abide our presence until we have been forgiven or washed clean, but rather that in his presence we can be transformed.

The victory of the cross

An historical alternative to the substitutionary atonement model is to say that the Devil in some way demands the price, and that by paying the price God gains the ultimate victory over the Devil.[71] C. S. Lewis uses that model in *The Lion, the Witch and the Wardrobe*, where the white witch demands that Edmund is handed over to her as his punishment for his betrayal of his family. Aslan offers himself instead, dying on the stone table, but the witch does not know the greater magic, which means that because Aslan is innocent, death cannot hold him, and he will rise again.[72] This type of model is known as *"Christus Victor"*. McGrath gives a wonderful quote from Rufinus of Aquileia in his exposition of the Apostles' Creed in 400 CE, describing Jesus' divine virtue as like a hook hidden beneath his human flesh. Just as a fish bites the flesh and is captured by the hook, so the Devil used the power of death to seize Jesus, only to find himself defeated.[73] The trouble with this model is that it suggests that the Devil, or evil, has a power that is on a par with God. This is known as dualism. But does that fit with God being the creator of everything, the name above all names?

At Durham we heard that Gustaf Aulén's book, *Christus Victor*,[74] renewed interest in the model. McGrath comments that the evil shown in the twentieth century, and Sigmund Freud's thesis that we are bound by destructive subconscious forces, gave new credence to the idea that there are forces of evil that need defeating. McGrath's criticism, which I agree with, was that Aulén gave no explanation of the way the forces of evil were defeated on the cross.[75]

Personally, I am convinced of the truth of God's victory on the cross. By looking at my own life, and historical events, I can see three distinct ways in which the cross really does defeat the forces of evil. When I remember the biblical events and the impact of Christianity over 2,000 years, then the victorious power of the cross is amazing, and radically different to normal forms of power.

Power to know that we are forgiven
In the story of Adam and Eve in the Garden of Eden, Adam and Eve's immediate reaction to God's presence after they have eaten the fruit is

to hide. I do not think that this is literal history, but it is a powerful and truthful description of temptation and the consequence of sin. When I do something that I know is wrong, my instinctive reaction is to try to cover it up or lie. I do that because I expect consequences. I don't like being told off. Alternatively, my other natural tactic would be to blame someone else, as Adam blamed Eve and Eve blamed the serpent.

However, it is different if we know that we can be forgiven. On the cross Jesus prayed, "Father, forgive them; for they do not know what they are doing" (Luke 23:34). Jesus suffered the worst injustice and violence the world could give. He was betrayed by a friend. He endured false charges made by those who were jealous of him and threatened by his influence. He was convicted when the judge knew he was innocent. The crowd who had shouted Hosanna changed to demand his crucifixion. He was whipped and ridiculed, and had a crown of thorns put on his head. He had nails driven through his wrists and his ankles and then died an agonizing death from suffocation when his muscles could no longer push up to enable him to breathe. And yet still he prayed, "Father, forgive them".

For much of history, people have lived in fear of God, worrying that if they do not do things right, they will be punished. Parts of the Old Testament and sometimes the Church have taught this as God's character, with threats of eternal damnation if people did not do what the Church wanted. Knowing that Jesus prayed for the forgiveness of those who killed him should surely break the power of that fear, and it breaks the power of the bullies who might manipulate that fear to their own ends. It affirms the core testimony of the Old Testament that God is the good shepherd, slow to anger and abounding in love.

As a child, I often behaved badly, including having fights with my brother, and caused my mother a lot of stress. I can remember being told off and storming off to bed having a temper tantrum. On the following morning on a couple of occasions I got up determined to carry on being grumpy, but when I came downstairs my mother's friendly voice came asking what I wanted for breakfast. My bad behaviour was forgiven, and my relationship restored.

Forgiveness in that sense always involves the one who suffers paying the price. The one who suffers is the sacrifice. The offer of forgiveness transforms the agony into a sacrifice or a ransom payment. In that sense, rather than a vengeful God demanding a sacrifice, the cross reveals the vengeful nature of humankind. We demanded that Jesus died, or did nothing to stop it. God did not exert his power by fighting back. He exerted his power by dying, accepting the injustice, and offering undeserved forgiveness in return. A sacrifice to vengeful humanity, exposing the evil, and responding with love. A power that changed hearts and minds.

Power to change minds and attitudes, exposing evil and good
When Jesus was crucified, one thief who was crucified next to him hurled insults at him, but the other thief responded:

> "Do you not fear God, since you are under the same sentence of condemnation? And we indeed have been condemned justly, for we are getting what we deserve for our deeds, but this man has done nothing wrong."
>
> *Luke 23:40–41*

After Jesus' death, the centurion who watched it said:

> "Certainly this man was innocent."
>
> *Luke 23:47*

Jesus' death changed them.

A few years later, Stephen was killed for his Christian faith. As he was being hit by the stones that ended his life he prayed: "Lord, do not hold this sin against them" (Acts 7:60). A young man called Saul was watching, beginning his persecution of the Church. My guess is that those words must have nagged at him. Why would Stephen pray so earnestly for forgiveness for Saul and the men hurling stones? Why did he show that love when Saul had deliberately played his part in killing Stephen and persecuting his friends in the Church? Those words and the look on Stephen's face must have paved the way for Saul's conversion a few weeks later. Saul became St Paul.

Mahatma Gandhi, in his protest against British oppression when India was part of the British Empire, refused to use violence. Similarly, Martin

Luther King insisted on non-violent protest in the civil rights movement against racism and discrimination. They were both, in part, inspired by Jesus on the cross. By protesting without violence, they exposed brutality and injustice, and changed hearts, minds and laws. That involved Gandhi and Martin Luther King exposing themselves to violence and not fighting back. It involved their followers doing the same. Both Gandhi and Martin Luther King were in the end killed for their actions. They paid the price. By following Jesus' example on the cross, they changed the world.

The power of the cross is in part its power to inspire others to follow Jesus' example. In the grand scope of history, the cross appears to be a small insignificant event—the death of one religious leader in an obscure country 2,000 years ago. But because people have shared the story and followed Jesus' example, the power of the cross has spread and transformed the world. There are those who call themselves Christians in every country on earth.

In Paul's case, he came to know how wrong he had been. He had tried to wipe out the Church. He had played his part in killing Stephen. But rather than receiving the punishment he deserved, he received amazing forgiveness. He wrote:

> For Jews demand signs and Greeks desire wisdom, but we proclaim Christ crucified, a stumbling-block to Jews and foolishness to Gentiles, but to those who are the called, both Jews and Greeks, Christ the power of God and the wisdom of God. For God's foolishness is wiser than human wisdom, and God's weakness is stronger than human strength.
>
> *1 Corinthians 1:22–25*

Power to end conflict

In 1987 a bomb planted by the Provisional IRA exploded during Enniskillen's Remembrance Day parade. Gordon Wilson was standing next to his daughter Marie when the bomb went off. They were both injured and buried in the rubble, and Marie died there. In an emotional interview on the BBC only hours later, Gordon stated: "I bear no ill will. I bear no grudge."[76] Gordon and Marie both paid the price in different ways, they both suffered, but Gordon's calls for forgiveness and reconciliation were, I believe, a significant part of the process which led to peace in Northern Ireland. For decades, both sides had pointed to the evils of the other as motivation for their violence and intransigence. Gordon Wilson played his part in cutting the Gordian Knot, and bringing peace that seemed impossible. The process, of course, needs to continue.

Nelson Mandela was imprisoned in South Africa for twenty-seven years for his part in opposing apartheid. But when he was eventually released to become the first black president of South Africa, he did not seek revenge, but reconciliation. He sought to expose and dismantle racism, with his truth and reconciliation agenda, but his purpose was to bring healing. He could not change the past, but by his forgiveness of his persecutors he changed the future.

At school I learnt how after the First World War, Britain and its allies demanded reparation from Germany. Some historians think that the cost and humiliation of those demands paved the way for the rise of Hitler and the Second World War. In contrast, after the Second World War, West Germany's economic recovery was enabled by payments from the United States as part of the Marshall Plan. The evils of the Nazi leaders were exposed and punished though the Nuremberg trials, but for the majority of Germany forgiveness was offered, paving the way for peace in Western Europe.

Isn't there more to the cross?

The power of the cross is displayed in the forgiveness explicitly offered to those who killed Jesus. By implication, that breaks the image held by many of a vengeful angry God. It is on the cross that God's character is revealed. As we share the story and follow Christ's example then each generation can know God's real character, and peace and reconciliation can increase. Evil can be defeated.

And yet, in coming to the above conclusions, my gut reaction is to say that the cross must be much more than that. Surely it is the most cosmic, metaphysical, crucial event of all time, changing the very nature of the universe itself? Surely it is so much more than the communication of God's character?

Perhaps my desire to understand the cross in spectacular metaphysical terms, changing the laws of spiritual justice for all time, is a way of distracting me from the extraordinary facts that we do know. God the Son died, and instead of fighting back suffered the agony, praying, "Father, forgive them". God the Father suffered the agony of the death of God the Son. But he didn't smite anyone with thunderbolts in revenge. Does my desire to interpret the cross in more mystical ways reflect the way I would love to change the world, rather than the way God chose to change the world?

When the angel Gabriel told Mary that she would give birth to God's son, he told her that she should give him the name Jesus, which means *God saves*. In Joseph's dream the angel's words to him were more explicit:

> [Y]ou are to name him Jesus, for he will save his people from their sins.
>
> *Matthew 1:21*

Jesus did not just come to bring forgiveness, but he came to save us.

That salvation is the most cosmic, metaphysical, crucial event of all time. It strikes me that the problem was not God's difficulty in forgiving but our difficulty in repenting. We need to be saved, not just forgiven.

More earthly than heavenly?

As I understand it, God was and is appalled at the sin he sees on earth. He is angry at the violence, selfishness and abuse. I believe he also weeps at the suffering, though I do not understand why he allows it. Jesus' coming to earth is how God responded to that horror. It was and is his way of putting things right, of bringing his healing.

The above reflects a significant shift in my own understanding of the cross. For years I have thought of the cross as being primarily about God offering us eternal life. The cross made it possible for me to go to heaven. John 3:16 does say that Jesus came that we might have eternal life. But the above analysis suggests that God's love for the world now, as we live in it, is equally important.

Which brings us to the next layer of thought—why did Jesus come?

CHAPTER 9

Why Did Jesus Come Part 1: The Kingdom of God

When I thought about the question of why Jesus came, the third verse of the old hymn *There is a Green Hill Far Away* came to mind:

> He died that we might be forgiven,
> He died to make us good,
> That we might go at last to Heaven,
> Saved by His precious blood.

In contrast John the Baptist declared:

> Repent, for the kingdom of heaven has come near.... I baptize you with water for repentance, but one who is more powerful than I is coming after me; I am not worthy to carry his sandals. He will baptize you with the Holy Spirit and fire.
>
> Matthew 3:2,11

I wrote in the last chapter of how I changed my understanding of Jesus' death on the cross: that it was not crucial in enabling God the Father to forgive, but rather that through the cross we can know that forgiveness. We can know the depth and breadth of God's love for us, and through that knowledge the chains of guilt and evil can be broken.

Sometimes in churches I have felt that people thought that Jesus came that we might be forgiven, and that was it. But forgiveness was the message of John the Baptist, and he was just preparing the way for someone so much more important.

Clearly forgiveness and eternal life were fundamental to Jesus' purpose, but John the Baptist did not mention either of them in connection with Jesus' arrival. Instead he spoke of the kingdom of God, and Jesus coming to baptize with the Holy Spirit and fire. So for this chapter: What did Jesus mean by the kingdom of God?

The meaning of the kingdom of God

Jesus began his public ministry echoing what John the Baptist said:

> "The time is fulfilled, and the kingdom of God has come near; repent, and believe in the good news."
>
> Mark 1:15

I cannot remember learning about the kingdom of God when I was growing up, but I can remember when I was about twenty hearing teaching on the subject for the first time. The following is a summary of what I was taught then, which has been reinforced in my subsequent studies.

Using my four sources for theology, Jesus' teaching in the Gospels is our primary source, but we need to use our reason, experience and other people to understand the significance of his words and actions.

Not a geographical kingdom

We were told that the kingdom of God is not a kingdom in a geographical sense like the United Kingdom. The kingdom of God is anywhere and everywhere that God's will is done. So parables about the kingdom of God also speak about how God wants to change the world so that his kingdom grows. When I had heard that, the parables made much more sense.

In Luke 4:18,19, Jesus uses a quotation from Isaiah to summarize why he came:

> The Spirit of the Lord is upon me, because he has anointed me to bring good news to the poor.

> He has sent me to proclaim release to the captives and
> recovery of sight to the blind, to let the oppressed
> go free, to proclaim the year of the Lord's favour.

God's kingdom comes, his will is done, when the poor receive good news, captives and the oppressed are set free, and the blind recover their sight.

Matthew's Gospel uses the phrase "the kingdom of Heaven" where Mark and Luke use "the kingdom of God". They mean the same thing. The Gospel authors have just used a different Greek phrase to translate the same Aramaic word. The phrase "kingdom of heaven" perhaps led to me thinking that Jesus' teaching concerned where we go when we die, but looking at the parables reveals that they are about so much more. They are about God's will being done on earth.

The mechanics of the kingdom of God: The Parable of the Mustard Seed

> With what can we compare the kingdom of God, or what parable will we use for it? It is like a mustard seed, which, when sown upon the ground, is the smallest of all the seeds on earth; yet when it is sown it grows up and becomes the greatest of all shrubs, and puts forth large branches, so that the birds of the air can make nests in its shade.
>
> *Mark 4:30-32*

The Parable of the Mustard Seed speaks of Jesus' earthly ministry. It seemed so small and insignificant compared to the great breadth of history, and yet it had extraordinary consequences. Jesus never had a position of political power. He never wrote a book. He was born in poverty and lived his first thirty years in obscurity. He had just three years of public ministry during which he never travelled more than about one hundred miles from where he was born. He died the death of a criminal and his followers failed to put up a fight. He seemed so small and insignificant, and yet Christianity is now a worldwide religion.

That growth of the Church is amazing, but there is more: because the parable is about the kingdom of God, it is not just about people calling themselves Christians. It is about God's will actually being done. It is easy to get depressed in our world today when we see the violence on our television screens or the internet, but it is good to think also about how much has changed over the last 2,000 years. When Jesus was alive it was normal for people to be killed for public entertainment in the gladiator ring. The Roman Empire grew by violence, and forcing people into slavery was common. In contrast, today we have internationally agreed human rights, the United Nations, and slavery is no longer legal. There is a long way to go, but in so many ways the world is a better place. Christians have been significant in many of those steps forward, though of course not exclusively.

In engineering, we learnt that the most efficient power stations only converted around 40 per cent of the energy in fossil fuels into electricity. You got out less than you put in. The inspiring nature of the Parable of the Mustard Seed is that you get out far more than you put in. In "chaos theory", a theoretical butterfly in China could change the weather in England. Many systems are inherently unstable so that a small change can have enormous results, as the Parable of the Mustard Seed shows. The kingdom of God starts by being small, appearing insignificant, but in time grows in a spectacular way.

The Parable of the Wheat and the Weeds

> The kingdom of heaven may be compared to someone who sowed good seed in his field; but while everybody was asleep, an enemy came and sowed weeds among the wheat, and then went away. So when the plants came up and bore grain, then the weeds appeared as well. And the slaves of the householder came and said to him, "Master, did you not sow good seed in your field? Where, then, did these weeds come from?" He answered, "An enemy has done this." The slaves said to him, "Then do you want us to go and gather them?" But he replied, "No; for in gathering the weeds you would uproot the wheat along with them. Let both of them grow together until the harvest; and at harvest time I will tell the

reapers, Collect the weeds first and bind them in bundles to be burned, but gather the wheat into my barn."

Matthew 13:24–30

The Parable of the Wheat and the Weeds is a powerful picture of how the kingdom grows amidst the reality of the world we see today. Just as the good seed grows, so bad weeds seem to be growing and becoming stronger. The development of technology means that one person can do vast amounts of harm. Our news can be depressing. This parable is one of hope, suggesting that the good seed can keep growing no matter what is going on around it. Digging up all the weeds might do more harm than good. As a gardener I am not always sure what are weeds and what are good plants, and sometimes you cannot dig up one without killing the other. In some way that we do not understand, it is God's purpose to allow the bad seed to grow for a time.

This was particularly significant for the context in which Jesus told the parables. At the time, the Jews were hoping for their Messiah—God's anointed leader. They expected him to be like another King David. The passages we read at Christmas carol services speak of his kingdom:

> For a child has been born for us, a son given to us; authority rests upon his shoulders; and he is named Wonderful Counsellor, Mighty God, Everlasting Father, Prince of Peace. His authority shall grow continually, and there shall be endless peace for the throne of David and his kingdom. He will establish and uphold it with justice and with righteousness from this time onwards and for evermore.
>
> *Isaiah 9:6,7*

So they expected their Messiah to raise up an army, drive out the Romans and restore Israel to be an independent respected nation as it had been in the time of David and Solomon. But Jesus taught:

> You have heard that it was said, "An eye for an eye and a tooth for a tooth." But I say to you, Do not resist an evildoer. But if anyone strikes you on the right cheek, turn the other also; and if anyone

> wants to sue you and take your coat, give your cloak as well; and if anyone forces you to go one mile, go also the second mile.
>
> Matthew 5:38–41

Jesus had not come to pull the weeds up with the violence of a normal gardener, or a military leader. He rejected the military model of King David and Goliath. Jesus' kingdom would grow by different means.

The kingdom of God involves a struggle between good and evil, but the method of struggle was to be radically different from the power struggles we see around us. The weeds look alarming, but we can have confidence that the good will grow, and in the end there will be cleansing or judgement.

The Parable of the Wedding Feast

> Someone gave a great dinner and invited many. At the time for the dinner he sent his slave to say to those who had been invited, "Come; for everything is ready now." But they all alike began to make excuses. The first said to him, "I have bought a piece of land, and I must go out and see it; please accept my apologies." Another said, "I have bought five yoke of oxen, and I am going to try them out; please accept my apologies." Another said, "I have just been married, and therefore I cannot come." So the slave returned and reported this to his master. Then the owner of the house became angry and said to his slave, "Go out at once into the streets and lanes of the town and bring in the poor, the crippled, the blind, and the lame." And the slave said, "Sir, what you ordered has been done, and there is still room." Then the master said to the slave, "Go out into the roads and lanes, and compel people to come in, so that my house may be filled. For I tell you, none of those who were invited will taste my dinner."
>
> Luke 14:16–24

The Pharisees of Jesus' time believed that the kingdom of God would come in some way when all the people of Israel were as pure and holy as the Pharisees tried to be. With good reason they thought, from their scriptures, that the fortunes of Israel were tied up with how good they were at obeying the Old Testament law:

> If you will only obey the Lord your God, by diligently observing all his commandments that I am commanding you today, the Lord your God will set you high above all the nations of the earth; all these blessings shall come upon you and overtake you, if you obey the Lord your God . . .
>
> *Deuteronomy 28:1–2*

At first they may have been hopeful that they could work with Jesus, but he shocked them by spending so much of his time with the so-called "sinners". As a result, the Pharisees and the chief priests turned away from Jesus, while the ordinary people and the sinners flocked to him. The parable speaks of the kingdom of God being like a banquet, where some will turn down the invitations, and instead the banquet will be full of unexpected guests. It speaks also of the kingdom growing by welcoming in those who are outside, rather than pursuing an isolationist "holiness". As such Jesus' teaching and actions also spoke of a radical change from the Jewish understanding of the Old Testament teaching.

The kingdom of God: now and not yet

Jesus said:

> [I]f it is by the Spirit of God that I cast out demons, then the kingdom of God has come to you.
>
> *Matthew 12:28*

There is much debate as to what is meant by casting out demons, but what we know for certain is that these events were characteristic of Jesus' ministry. In this quotation Jesus is therefore saying that those exorcisms are a sign that God's kingdom has come.

However, the sayings that the kingdom of God has come have to be balanced with those that speak of the kingdom growing, like the parables of the mustard seed and of the weeds, and those that speak of the banquet and judgement in the future. The explanation that I was taught, and that makes sense to me, is that:

- With Jesus' public ministry the kingdom came in the form of the small seed that started growing.
- We are currently in the growing phase of the kingdom, with the wheat and the weeds growing together.
- One day, Jesus will come again, and the kingdom will be completed.

The kingdom is "now" but also "not yet".

In engineering terms, it is perhaps like electric cars. One day internal combustion engines will have to disappear, if we are to combat global warming. Electric cars are the future, but they are also available now for those who want to use them.

Jesus' death and the kingdom of God

The Old Covenant and the New Covenant

As well as learning about the kingdom of God, the other key term I have learnt for understanding the New Testament is the word "covenant". Covenant and testament in this context mean the same thing.

In Abraham's time, in a covenant a stronger tribe would promise protection and help to a weaker tribe in return for soldiers or payment. It was seen as a solemn promise sealed with the shedding of animal blood. In the Old Testament, God made a covenant with Abraham. God promised Abraham that he would make him the father of a great nation, a blessing to all nations, and that he would give his descendants the promised land (Genesis 12:1–3; 15:1–21). In return, Abraham had to obey God and leave his home country. God was true to his word, and Abraham's descendants became numerous. Moses brought them out of slavery in Egypt, and God then renewed the covenant with the whole nation, now called Israel. The covenant promised God's blessing and protection, if only the people would obey the law. The Old Testament, then, is largely a description of the failure of the Old Covenant, with God being faithful to his part and the people of Israel failing to keep theirs.

But Jeremiah prophesied:

> The days are surely coming, says the Lord, when I will make a *new covenant* with the house of Israel and the house of Judah. It will not be like the covenant that I made with their ancestors... I will put my law within them, and I will write it on their hearts; and I will be their God, and they shall be my people. No longer shall they teach one another, or say to each other, "Know the Lord", for they shall all know me, from the least of them to the greatest, says the Lord; for I will forgive their iniquity, and remember their sin no more. [my italics]
>
> *Jeremiah 31:31–34*

In Old Testament times, the Jews kept breaking the covenant. It was a failure. But it prepared the way for the New Covenant, God's new way of bringing his kingdom.

At the Last Supper, the final meal Jesus ate with his disciples before he died, Jesus

> took a cup, and after giving thanks he gave it to them, saying, "Drink from it, all of you; for this is my blood of the covenant, which is poured out for many for the forgiveness of sins".
>
> *Matthew 26:27,28*

Jesus came to bring a New Covenant. In the Old Covenant, forgiveness was offered through animal sacrifice. Now forgiveness is offered through Jesus. In the Old Covenant, the laws were vast and complicated, multiplied by tradition. In the New Covenant, the disciples were commanded to love as Jesus loved, including turning the other cheek. They were to be witnesses to what they had seen and heard and were to make disciples.

Under the Old Covenant, God promised that if Israel obeyed his laws, he would bless them and protect them. Under the New Covenant, promises connected to commands included:

> If you keep my commandments, you will abide in my love, just as I have kept my Father's commandments and abide in his love. I have said these things to you so that my joy may be in you, and that your joy may be complete. This is my commandment, that you love one another as I have loved you.... You did not choose me, but I chose you. And I appointed you to go and bear fruit, fruit that will last, so that the Father will give you whatever you ask him in my name. I am giving you these commands so that you may love one another.
>
> *John 15:10–12,16,17*

Commands and promises with the shedding of blood is symbolically a covenant. If the disciples obeyed, if they went on abiding in his love, they would bear fruit and would do greater things than Jesus did.

On occasion, I have said that if I were God, I would sort out some of the problems in the world with well-aimed thunderbolts. The Old Testament depicts that policy as not working. In the Old Testament, there are many occasions when the people of Israel appear willing to obey God because of terror. But the obedience never lasts. God does not want people just to obey him through fear. That would be a horrendous form of tyranny.

Jesus' coming, and inaugurating God's rule on earth in a new way, was and is God's response to the horrors we see around us. The physical healings, the emotional healings and the healed relationships that Jesus brought while he was on earth, are like the first fruits of a harvest. The key, however, for his kingdom to grow was and is Jesus' followers. In theory we should be seeing more fruit as the Church continues what Jesus began.

How does God's kingdom grow now?

I was shocked when I first noticed Jesus' words that I have quoted above, that the disciples would do what Jesus had been doing and would do greater things. Jesus had healed the sick, raised the dead, fed 5,000 and turned many lives upside down. How could the disciples possibly do what he had been doing? How could they do greater things? In engineering terms, "how does that work?"

On reflection, it struck me that the disciples doing what Jesus did was the heart of the difference between the Old and New Covenant. The disciples were not just to survive as a closed country, protecting themselves from the evil culture around them. As Jesus came from the Father into the world, so the disciples were to go from Jesus into the world.

In Jewish culture, a disciple did not merely learn from his teacher, his rabbi. The aim of a disciple was to become like his teacher, to imitate him. For the original disciples, and for us in our turn, the kingdom comes when we become disciples, continuing what Jesus began. But how could they do what Jesus did? Jesus was and is the Son of God, whereas we are mere mortals. Jesus said to his disciples shortly before ascending into heaven:

> You are witnesses of these things. And see, I am sending upon you what my Father promised; so stay here in the city until you have been clothed with power from on high.
>
> *Luke 24:48,49*

And from the "farewell discourses" in John's Gospel:

> I tell you the truth: it is to your advantage that I go away, for if I do not go away, the Advocate will not come to you; but if I go, I will send him to you.
>
> *John 16:7*

The power that Jesus promises in Luke, and the Advocate in John, refer to the coming of the Spirit. As John the Baptist said, Jesus would come to baptize with the Holy Spirit and with fire. Jesus' life, death and resurrection were crucial for the coming of the Spirit, and the coming of the Spirit was crucial for the next stage of the coming of the kingdom of God.

CHAPTER 10

Why Did Jesus Come Part 2: The Holy Spirit

In my childhood experience of church, I can remember very little teaching about the Holy Spirit. I recall celebrating Pentecost every year. We heard about the Spirit coming on the disciples, the sound of wind and tongues of fire, and the disciples sharing the good news in the languages of all those present in Jerusalem that day. But my memory of those celebrations is that we were remembering an event that happened nearly 2,000 years ago, rather than an event that has significant implications for us now. I do not remember any teaching about what John the Baptist might have meant when he said that Jesus would baptize with the Holy Spirit and with fire.

Then when I was around sixteen years old, I became involved in my school Christian Union, and in an ecumenical renewal movement in Birmingham. By that I mean that the movement involved Christians from many different churches and that they put a significant emphasis on the work of the Holy Spirit. Since then I have had a rich, and at times painful, experience of a variety of churches and a variety of attitudes to the work of the Holy Spirit. In what follows I will try and share some key elements of my journey and how I have come to my present understanding.

Going back to my engineering analogies, I have come to my conclusions by using my four "sources". I have tried to use my reason, to understand what God has revealed in scripture, enlightened by my own experiences, and by the experiences and wisdom of others who have been part of my journey.

Also using my engineer's approach, I start with what I consider to be the solid foundations of things we can agree on, and from those foundations I move on to more disputable secondary matters where I hope we can all be happy to be tolerant.

The importance of the Holy Spirit

Starting with revelation, as the primary source for our theology, John the Baptist declared:

> Repent, for the kingdom of heaven has come near . . . I baptize you with water for repentance, but one who is more powerful than I is coming after me; I am not worthy to carry his sandals. He will baptize you with the Holy Spirit and fire.
>
> *Matthew 3:2,11*

Then from the farewell discourse in John's Gospel, where Jesus is preparing his disciples for his departure:

> I tell you the truth: it is to your advantage that I go away, for if I do not go away, the Advocate will not come to you; but if I go, I will send him to you.
>
> *John 16:7*

And from Luke, Jesus says to his disciples before ascending into heaven:

> You are witnesses of these things. And see, I am sending upon you what my Father promised; so stay here in the city until you have been clothed with power from on high.
>
> *Luke 24:48,49*

I hope it is clear from these verses that the Holy Spirit is crucial. John the Baptist's prophecy that Jesus would baptize with the Holy Spirit and with fire was the only thing he said about what Jesus was coming to do. Jesus himself was then specific in telling his disciples that the Holy Spirit was necessary and that they should wait for him.

Moving on to Acts 2, the significance is obvious. The disciples were transformed. Instead of hiding behind locked doors, they threw the doors open. Instead of getting things wrong, Peter got things right, and 3,000 were added to the Church that day.

These scriptural accounts, as primary sources of information, tell us that the work of the Holy Spirit is vital. Few Christians would dispute that. However, it is not so clear how and when the Spirit works, and in my experience over the years, there have been significant amounts of disagreement on this topic.

Who is the Spirit?

Some of the teaching I heard as a teenager reflected the "power" language of Luke 24, quoted above. The Holy Spirit was like electricity. But in the farewell discourses of John 14 to 16, Jesus paints a different picture of the Holy Spirit:

> If you love me, you will keep my commandments. And I will ask the Father, and he will give you another Advocate, to be with you for ever. This is the Spirit of truth, whom the world cannot receive, because it neither sees him nor knows him. You know him, because he abides with you, and he will be in you.
>
> I will not leave you orphaned; I am coming to you. In a little while the world will no longer see me, but you will see me; because I live, you also will live. On that day you will know that I am in my Father, and you in me, and I in you.
>
> *John 14:15–20*

The passage is confusing. Jesus said that he was going and that in his place the Father would send the Advocate, the Spirit of truth. But then he said that he would come to the disciples, and that they would live in him as he lives in his Father. Was Jesus going away and sending the Spirit in his place, or was he coming back to be with the disciples?

The Church has used reason as a source for interpreting these passages and has come to the answer that Jesus was talking about God as Trinity. He was not talking about three separate gods, but that God is both three and one. His departure, and the Spirit coming in his place, indicated a change in the nature of the disciples' relationship with God the Trinity. Jesus' statement that he and the Father would come indicates that underneath that change, his relationship with the disciples would continue.

Thus the simplest answer to the question, "Who is the Spirit?" is that the Holy Spirit is God himself, a part of the Trinity. He is much more than a source of power. It is impossible to find language to adequately describe the relationship. Sometimes it is easiest to talk about the Holy Spirit in relation to the Father and Son as if they were three gods, but in doing so we must also always remember they are one.

Jesus' death and the coming of the Holy Spirit

In the previous chapters, I asked why Jesus had to die, and concluded that it was fundamental to bringing God's kingdom and defeating evil. In the beginning of this chapter I quoted the passages from Luke and Acts where Jesus said that the disciples should wait in Jerusalem for the coming of the Spirit so that they could be clothed with power from on high. They needed to wait before they could continue the work Jesus began.

This leads me to the question, "Why did they have to wait?" Why didn't God just clothe people with power earlier to grow the kingdom of God? Why didn't he do it when Jesus first called his followers? Why was it that it followed Jesus' death, resurrection and ascension?

As the question occurred to me, in writing this book, I looked at a number of New Testament theologies and discovered that they did not seem to ask the question. Only in Gordon Fee's *God's Empowering Presence* did I find part of the answer I was looking for. Fee's answer was that the Holy Spirit was crucial for conversion. Conversion involves:

> A clearly subjective experiential appropriation that results in some radical changes in the believer; and the Spirit is the absolutely crucial element for this dimension of conversion.[77]

Fee particularly refers to Paul's statements about us becoming God's children:

> God sent his Son, born of a woman, born under the law, in order to redeem those who were under the law, so that we might receive adoption as children. And because you are children, God has sent the Spirit of his Son into our hearts, crying, 'Abba! Father!'
> *Galatians 4:4–6*

> [Y]ou did not receive a spirit of slavery to fall back into fear, but you have received a spirit of adoption. When we cry, 'Abba! Father!' it is that very Spirit bearing witness with our spirit that we are children of God, and if children, then heirs, heirs of God and joint heirs with Christ—if, in fact, we suffer with him so that we may also be glorified with him.
> *Romans 8:15–17*

Our adoption as God's children

Considering this, our adoption as God's children is at the heart of the Gospel, and fundamental to why Jesus came and died on the cross. In striking contrast to Old Testament language for God, Jesus declared that we should call God, "Abba". "Abba" is the Aramaic word, often translated as "father", but might be translated as "daddy". "Abba" was the title for an intimate address of a son to his father, not childish as "daddy", not informal as "dad", not formal as "father", but a loving, respectful intimate combination of the three. According to Paul in the quotations above, the Holy Spirit enables us to know or experience this adoption. Jesus in John 14, quoted above, said that he would "not leave them as orphans".

In the Prologue to John's Gospel, words I read out every Christmas:

> But to all who received him, who believed in his name, he gave power to become children of God.
> *John 1:12*

As I write I am thinking of a number of families I know where children have been adopted. I think of details I know of the awful situation some of those children were in before they were adopted, and the wonderful sight of them being with new parents.

In the Parable of the Prodigal Son (Luke 15:11–32), the older son resents the younger son coming home and being welcomed into the family. In contrast, Jesus' life and death demonstrated that he was quite the opposite, longing to expand the family and share his inheritance. In a more modern parallel, in Mark Stibbe's *My Father's Tears* he writes of his own adoption, and of the welcome from his adopted father's son.[78]

By his life, death and resurrection Jesus gave the invitation to us to become God's children. With the coming of the Spirit, that invitation became an experienced reality. In the Old Testament we can read of the Holy Spirit at work with individuals, giving Bezalel the artistic skills he needed for work on the first tabernacle (Exodus 31:2,3), enabling prophets to prophesy (1 Samuel 10:6–10) and leaders to rule (Judges 3:10).

The difference with the coming of the Spirit in Acts 2 is not just that the Spirit was poured out on so many, but also that they could know God as their Father. They could begin to taste the reality of being children of God.

Baptism in the Holy Spirit

This doctrine of the Trinity and the work of the Spirit in our adoption reflects the widespread understanding of the Church—the sources of revelation, reason and other people combining to provide a consensus. But there has been significant disagreement when experience is included as a source for our understanding of what the Holy Spirit does.

John the Baptist spoke of Jesus coming so that we might be baptized in the Holy Spirit. But what did he mean by the phrase "baptism in the Holy Spirit"? How do we know if we have been baptized in the Holy Spirit? Does it include specific experiences?

Many people have had particular experiences, connected with their conversion or other significant points in their Christian lives. How do these experiences relate to the Holy Spirit?

In Acts 2, when the Spirit came upon the disciples on the day of Pentecost, there was a sound like wind, the house shook and tongues of fire rested upon the disciples. They then spoke in the different languages of those who were in Jerusalem that day.

Later in Acts there are three other instances where the Spirit comes upon a group for the first time:

> Now when the apostles at Jerusalem heard that Samaria had accepted the word of God, they sent Peter and John to them. The two went down and prayed for them that they might receive the Holy Spirit (for as yet the Spirit had not come upon any of them; they had only been baptized in the name of the Lord Jesus). Then Peter and John laid their hands on them, and they received the Holy Spirit.
>
> Acts 8:14–17

> While Peter was still speaking, the Holy Spirit fell upon all who heard the word. The circumcised believers who had come with Peter were astounded that the gift of the Holy Spirit had been poured out even on the Gentiles, for they heard them speaking in tongues and extolling God.
>
> Acts 10:44–46

> Paul passed through the inland regions and came to Ephesus, where he found some disciples. He said to them, 'Did you receive the Holy Spirit when you became believers?' They replied, 'No, we have not even heard that there is a Holy Spirit.' Then he said, 'Into what then were you baptized?' They answered, 'Into John's baptism.' Paul said, 'John baptized with the baptism of repentance, telling the people to believe in the one who was to come after him, that is, in Jesus.' On hearing this, they were baptized in the name of the Lord Jesus. When Paul had laid his hands on them,

the Holy Spirit came upon them, and they spoke in tongues and
prophesied—altogether there were about twelve of them.

Acts 19:1–7

One answer as to what is meant by baptism in the Spirit has been provided by the Pentecostal movement. The teaching of classical Pentecostalism is that Baptism in the Spirit is always accompanied by "speaking in tongues". The Greek word translated as "tongues" means languages, but the word tongues has been adopted for where the Holy Spirit enables people to speak in a language unknown to them. In two of the three instances above we are told that the believers spoke in tongues on receiving the Spirit, and in the third case the results of receiving the Spirit were obvious to those present. In the beginning of the Pentecostal movement, Christians started speaking in tongues, particularly during the Azusa Street revival in 1906. The Pentecostal teachers used their reason to combine these scriptures with their experiences to develop their theology. The Assemblies of God is one of the main branches of the Pentecostal Church in the United Kingdom, and their statement of belief includes:

> We believe in the baptism in the Holy Spirit as an enduement of the believer with power for service, the essential, biblical evidence of which is the speaking with other tongues as the Spirit gives utterance.[79]

When I was a teenager, I encountered this teaching that the sign of being baptized in the Spirit was speaking in tongues. As a result, I longed to speak in tongues, possibly because of spiritual vanity. I was taught that speaking in tongues could sometimes be in an earthly language that some other people could understand, but more commonly it would be the "language of angels", as Paul mentions in 1 Corinthians 13.

However, the counter argument to this teaching is to note that Paul in 1 Corinthians 12 clearly states that speaking in tongues is just one of many potential "gifts" of the Spirit. By "gifts" he means special abilities given to Christians by God. Paul states that speaking in tongues is one of lesser importance:

> Now there are varieties of gifts, but the same Spirit; and there are varieties of services, but the same Lord....
>
> For just as the body is one and has many members, and all the members of the body, though many, are one body, so it is with Christ....
>
> If the whole body were an eye, where would the hearing be? If the whole body were hearing, where would the sense of smell be?
>
> Are all apostles? Are all prophets? Are all teachers? Do all work miracles? Do all possess gifts of healing? Do all speak in tongues? Do all interpret? But strive for the greater gifts.
>
> 1 Corinthians 12:4,12,17,29-31

Paul clearly states that speaking in tongues is just one amongst many manifestations of the Holy Spirit.

In addition, in Acts 2 the form of speaking in tongues involved languages that others could understand. If Acts 2 is to be seen as definitive of Baptism in the Spirit then it should surely include this type of speaking in tongues, and possibly tongues of fire, wind and buildings shaking.

Thus, taking into account the breadth of scripture, and using my reason, I cannot agree with the Assemblies of God statement. I do, however, want to honour the work of the Pentecostal movement in reigniting interest in the work of the Holy Spirit. I think that their combination of scripture and their experience is valid in showing that the Holy Spirit may give supernatural gifts to Christians today, including speaking in tongues. I do think that our experience is a valid source for our theology, but it must be used with caution.

It is why it is important to look at what the Bible says as a whole, rather than just a few passages, and why it is also good to listen to others who may have had different and complementary experiences.

With that in mind it is also important to note that there are a number of different lists of gifts of the Spirit. The fact that they differ says to me that they are not meant to be complete lists. I love the fact that some of the gifts are very "ordinary":

> We have gifts that differ according to the grace given to us: prophecy, in proportion to faith; ministry, in ministering; the

teacher, in teaching; the exhorter, in exhortation; the giver, in generosity; the leader, in diligence; the compassionate, in cheerfulness.

Romans 12:6–8

My baptism in the Spirit?

In Jesus' baptism, the Spirit came down and alighted on Jesus like a dove (Matthew 3:16,17). Then the Father's voice is heard saying, "this is my Son, the Beloved, with whom I am well pleased". As Jesus' baptism included the coming of the Spirit, it strikes me that "Baptism in the Spirit" must in some way be similar. But I don't know anyone who has seen the Holy Spirit coming down like a dove, or heard an audible voice declaring that we are God's children.

For my own understanding of what it means to be baptized in the Spirit I combine the above passages from Acts, the account of Jesus' baptism, my own varied experiences and conversations with others:

As I mentioned earlier, when I was about ten years old, I tried to pray for the first time, and had the sense that God picked up the other end of the telephone line. I did not hear audible voices, but I sensed that God loved me like a Father. Was that my baptism in the Spirit?

When I was seventeen years old, I went on a Christian holiday with other teenagers. We had talks about the basics of the Christian faith. A friend who had been going to these holidays for a few years asked me what I thought of it. With the arrogance of a teenage grammar school child, I said that I had heard it all before and I was a bit bored. With a frankness that I found shocking, but I now appreciate, she asked me why I did not put it into practice! I had started the holiday with my girlfriend of eight months, and my behaviour had not always been good. We split up during the holiday. Hence the comment about putting it into practice. On the last night of the holiday we had a meeting where we could share things we had learnt during the week. I stood up and I said that I had learnt that I was a hypocrite. It was the first time I had done something that I thought God wanted me to do without wanting something in return. During the songs that followed it was the first time I had ever wanted to sing to God and express emotionally what he had done for me. But I had a problem—I had been told I couldn't sing. My voice had broken when I was young and after a couple of uncomplimentary remarks I had rarely sung since. I knew that when I tried it did not sound right. That night I did not speak in tongues, but I did sing, and it sounded OK to me. I also had a sense that God was there in a way that I had never known before. Was that my baptism in the Spirit?

About eighteen months later when I was having a "quiet time"—a time of prayer that I got round to at varying intervals—I found myself doing what I think is speaking in tongues. This was not an earthly language as far as I know. I have continued to do so at times over the years as part of private prayer, especially when I feel I have run out of words or do not know how to pray. Was that my baptism in the Spirit?

I have also had contact with a number of people over the years who have longed for some experience as an affirmation of their relationship with God. In these cases they were all "godly" people, who had a sound faith which they put into practice in their lives. But they did not have the sort of experience they were seeking.

Words of Paul that I have mentioned above have helped me as my understanding has developed:

> [A]ll who are led by the Spirit of God are children of God. For you did not receive a spirit of slavery to fall back into fear, but you have received a spirit of adoption. When we cry, 'Abba! Father!' it is that very Spirit bearing witness with our spirit that we are children of God.
>
> Romans 8:14–16

I believe that my prayer for help at ten years old began my active relationship with God as Father. My experiences, prayer life and Bible reading since then have deepened that relationship. When I think of my relationship with my earthly father, in some ways it has been similar. There have been many times as a child when he has picked me up, and I have enjoyed his physical presence. But those were not the occasions that have drawn us closest on a deep level. My relationship with my father is the result of a long journey, with some conversations and experiences that were particularly significant, but only as part of the whole journey. It would not be much of a relationship if it only involved experiences from long ago.

Which brings me to another verse that is important for me. Jesus said:

> Abide in me as I abide in you. Just as the branch cannot bear fruit by itself unless it abides in the vine, neither can you unless you abide in me.
>
> *John 15:4*

The idea of abiding with Jesus speaks to me of the importance of an ongoing relationship. It cannot just depend on how the relationship began. Rather than worrying about whether we have had a particular experience in the past, it seems to me that it is more important to concentrate on the present.

Trouble with spiritual experiences

It is also important to note that St Paul had significant problems with some who claimed to have had spiritual experiences:

> [S]ince you are eager for spiritual gifts, strive to excel in them for building up the church.... When you come together, each one has a hymn, a lesson, a revelation, a tongue, or an interpretation. Let all things be done for building up. If anyone speaks in a tongue, let there be only two or at most three, and each in turn; and let one interpret. But if there is no one to interpret, let them be silent in church and speak to themselves and to God.... for God is a God not of disorder but of peace.
>
> *1 Corinthians 14:12,26–28, 33*

> Do not despise the words of prophets, but test everything; hold fast to what is good; abstain from every form of evil.
>
> *1 Thessalonians 5:20–22*

The church in Corinth professed to be very spiritual, with their displays of spiritual gifts. But it was a church riven with division and ungodly behaviour.

In the churches that I have worked in, I have known a couple of people who talked of their spiritual experiences but who caused division. I have also come to know many people who would talk of their relationship with God as being no more than that sense that I had as a ten-year-old that God was there. They have shown their faith in their lives.

Jesus said:

> Beware of false prophets, who come to you in sheep's clothing but inwardly are ravenous wolves. You will know them by their fruits. Are grapes gathered from thorns, or figs from thistles? In the same way, every good tree bears good fruit, but the bad tree bears bad fruit. A good tree cannot bear bad fruit, nor can a bad tree bear good fruit.
>
> *Matthew 7:15–18*

In engineering, a design process might be described as "suck it and see"— in cooking, the only way to tell if a recipe works is to taste it, so also in engineering. Sometimes the only way to discover whether a design works is to build a prototype and try it. So my answer to whether the Spirit is at work is to "suck it and see"—do we see good fruit?

Paul describes the fruit of the Spirit as being:

> [L]ove, joy, peace, patience, kindness, generosity, faithfulness, gentleness, and self-control.
>
> *Galatians 5:22,23*

In Acts 2, the fruit of the Spirit at work was that many were set free from their guilt in killing Jesus, 3,000 became Christians, and people who spoke a vast range of languages ended up sharing their possessions. The biblical test for the work of the Holy Spirit is not whether we have had a particular experience, but whether we know God as our Father, and whether that makes a difference in our lives.

What did John the Baptist mean by baptism in the Spirit? The short answer is: "I still do not know". Scripture does not spell it out, my experiences are inconclusive, and the understanding of wise people over the centuries is varied. Reason, therefore, suggests that we should be flexible in our understanding, and allow for the Spirit to work in whatever way he chooses.

However, I believe we can say for certain that the work of the Holy Spirit is vital for our relationship with God as our Father, and for our work in continuing what Jesus began. The test for whether the Spirit is at work is whether good fruits are grown.

CHAPTER 11

The Spirit Leading the Disciples into all Truth

Wonderful engineering could easily be wrecked by poor instructions, and not just engineering. I have heard many complaints of flat-pack furniture let down by incomprehensible diagrams. So perhaps because of my background in engineering, when I left my last church, I gave the leaders instructions as to how to take services and what to do in various situations until my successor was appointed. If I were Jesus, I would have done the same for the disciples before ascending into heaven. I would have given them a new book of Leviticus.

Instead, Jesus said to the disciples as he prepared them for his departure:

> I still have many things to say to you, but you cannot bear them now. When the Spirit of truth comes, he will guide you into all the truth.
>
> *John 16:12,13*

Part of the significance of this statement is revealed in Acts 10, when Peter first took the Gospel to the Gentiles.

From Peter's understanding of Leviticus, he would only eat meat from certain animals, and they had to be killed in the right way. But as he was praying, he had a vision of a sheet coming down from heaven covered with all sorts of animals, and three times he heard a voice command him to kill and eat. Each time Peter refused, and the voice replied:

> What God has made clean, you must not call profane.
>
> *Acts 10:15*

Immediately afterwards a group of Gentiles came to his house saying that their master Cornelius had seen a vision, telling him to go and get Peter. Normally Peter would have refused to go with them because Jews considered Gentiles unclean, but because of his vision, Peter went. As he was sharing his faith, Acts tells us that the Holy Spirit came down upon the Gentiles as it had come down upon the disciples on the day of Pentecost.

Peter and the Early Church began to see that they were to lay aside the laws of Leviticus concerning diet and circumcision. Through Peter's and Cornelius' visions, and the Holy Spirit coming on the Gentiles, they were led into a radically different understanding of God's will.

In setting aside the dietary restrictions and circumcision, the Church was making the most extraordinary change. Circumcision had been the mark of what it meant to follow God from the time of Abraham. The dietary laws went back to Moses. They were the foundation of how the Jews lived their lives, believing that these rules came directly from God himself. These rules are also a significant part of our Bibles. Dispensing with those commands would be a bit like telling an engineer he could forget Newton's laws of motion. Looking back from the twenty-first century, it is almost impossible to appreciate the incredible, revolutionary nature of what the Early Church did.

But Jesus did not tell them in advance. In fact, he seems to say the opposite:

> [I]t is easier for heaven and earth to pass away, than for one stroke of a letter in the law to be dropped.
>
> *Luke 16:17*

And in Matthew:

> [T]ruly I tell you, until heaven and earth pass away, not one letter, not one stroke of a letter, will pass from the law until all is accomplished.
>
> *Matthew 5:18*

Instead of giving instructions when he was with them in the flesh, he left it to the Holy Spirit. And when the Spirit led Peter into this new truth, he did it when Peter was alone. He did not tell all the rest of the disciples at the same time. I would have done it differently.

How did the Church discern where the Spirit was leading?

In Acts 15, the Council of Jerusalem debated whether the Gentiles should be required to obey the whole law. Given my approach of using four sources for theology, I found it fascinating to see how the Council of Jerusalem came to their conclusions.

They started with what they considered God's revelation, with Christians who were also Pharisees saying:

> It is necessary for them to be circumcised and ordered to keep the law of Moses.
>
> *Acts 15:5*

Peter responded by telling his story, including his experience of revelation from God. Paul and Barnabas reinforced Peter's words with their own accounts of how Gentiles became Christians without obeying the law. Key to their argument is Peter's observation that the Holy Spirit came down on the Gentiles without them obeying the laws. The conclusion they reached was put in a letter to the Gentiles:

> For it has seemed good to the Holy Spirit and to us to impose on you no further burden than these essentials: that you abstain

> from what has been sacrificed to idols and from blood and from what is strangled and from fornication.
>
> *Acts 15:28,29*

Reading through the whole chapter, it appears that the council was a good model for listening, combining reason, experience and their understanding of God's revelation through the Holy Spirit. What is more uncomfortable for me is that God's revelation to Peter, and their combined experience and reason, in the end overcame their understanding of God's commands in the Old Testament.

Given the radical nature of the change and the Holy Spirit only speaking to Peter and the small number that witnessed the Spirit coming on the Gentiles, it is not surprising that they disagreed. Paul's letters show that the argument continued for many years.

Is the Spirit still leading us into all Truth?

My next question is whether the Holy Spirit stopped leading the Church into truth when the New Testament was finished and that first generation of disciples died. The traditional evangelical view is that he did stop then.[80] But I do not agree. Yes the majority of the work was done by then, but I think that the Spirit has continued to lead us into truth.

For example, Paul never told masters to set their slaves free. In his letter to Philemon about the runaway slave Onesimus, Paul asks Philemon to set Onesimus free as a favour, not because slavery is an evil monstrosity. I am told that in the parliamentary debates about the abolition of legalized slavery, the Bible was quoted more frequently in favour of keeping slavery than in favour of ending it. I believe that the Spirit led the Church to abolish slavery. Jesus hinted at it, when he said that he had come to set captives free, but it took the Church 1,800 years to understand.

The nature of the Bible—Static or alive and active?

The fact that the Spirit led the Early Church into such a radical change concerning the Old Testament law has consequences for how I view the Bible. I once pictured the Bible as static, full of instructions for all time.

That feels like a safe and solid foundation for life. But the Spirit led the Church to set aside so much of the Old Testament law—laws that were therefore not God's commands for all time. The Old Testament is thus revealed as more like a signpost, pointing in the right direction. If the Spirit is still leading us into all truth, are parts of the New Testament also signposts to the direction we should take rather than God's final word on a subject?

For example, what about Paul's teaching on slavery? What about Paul's teaching on the role of women in the Church?

Slavery in the New Testament
In Colossians 4:1 we read:

> Masters, treat your slaves justly and fairly, for you know that you also have a Master in heaven.

Tom Wright comments:

> This is every bit as revolutionary as what people today often wish he had said—that slaves should be freed at once (which was unthinkable in his day, where slaves did much of the work done today by gas, electricity and the internal combustion engine). Rather than dreaming of impossible freedoms, he prefers to offer practical guidelines.[81]

I understand Wright to be arguing that Paul's instructions were appropriate for that time, where abolishing slavery might have done more harm than good.

Jesus said:

> The Spirit of the Lord is upon me, because he has anointed me to bring good news to the poor. He has sent me to proclaim release to the captives and recovery of sight to the blind, to let the oppressed go free, to proclaim the year of the Lord's favour.
> Luke 4:18,19

My understanding is that Paul had not grasped the full extent of the revolution Jesus came to bring. Abolishing slavery was not top of Jesus' list of priorities 2,000 years ago, in that he didn't give explicit instructions for the Early Church. He left it for the Holy Spirit to lead us into all truth, and that journey was not complete when the New Testament was finished. Paul's teaching is a step in the right direction, but not the end of the journey. The Spirit had not finished leading him into all truth.

If we can say that about Paul's writing on slavery, then I think it is equally reasonable to set aside Paul's restrictive teaching on women. Paul wrote:

> As in all the churches of the saints, women should be silent in the churches. For they are not permitted to speak, but should be subordinate, as the law also says. If there is anything they desire to know, let them ask their husbands at home. For it is shameful for a woman to speak in church.
>
> *1 Corinthians 14:33–35*

However, he also wrote:

> There is no longer Jew or Greek, there is no longer slave or free, there is no longer male and female; for all of you are one in Christ Jesus.
>
> *Galatians 3:28*

Paul also wrote of Priscilla and Aquila as co-workers for Christ (Romans 16:3), and in Acts Philip has four daughters who were prophets (Acts 21:9). It is unlikely that as co-workers or prophets they remained silent.

These mixed references to the role of women in the Early Church suggest that Paul was on a journey, with the statement that all are one in Christ a step in the direction the Spirit was leading. This provides the biblical foundation for the Church setting aside the restrictions of the verses from 1 Corinthians quoted above. However, in writing this, am I treating these words of Paul as the Word of God?

In my first draft of this chapter, I expressed this by writing that I thought Paul was wrong. A colleague responded:

Was he wrong? Or was he viewing things the way a man of his epoch could?

As I wrote in chapter 6, for those from a less evangelical background, I hope that you can understand the caution I have in writing that Paul might be wrong, or that Paul might not have been led into all truth. In Genesis 3, the serpent asks Eve, "Did God say?" For most of the history of the Church we have considered the Bible to be the Word of God. Am I, like the serpent, asking "Did God *really* say"?

In 2 Timothy 3:16 we read that all scripture is inspired by God and is useful for teaching, reproof, correction and training in righteousness. Does that have to mean that the Old Testament and Paul were right about everything?

The Gospels clearly show that the disciples got things wrong, and yet God worked through them. They were on a journey, learning on the way.

I see that as a biblical argument for saying Paul's writing might sometimes reflect that discipleship process, rather than being the final word.

Why didn't Jesus tell them in advance?

Which leaves me with a question I still struggle with. Why didn't Jesus tell the disciples in advance about dropping the requirements of circumcision and diet? Jesus said: "Blessed be the peacemakers." If you want to referee a football match, and to avoid conflict, then the obvious thing to do is to tell everyone the rules in advance. Jesus' policy of leaving it to the Holy Spirit to lead the disciples into all truth seems to be a recipe for trouble.

And trouble and division has occurred in the Church ever since. In the early centuries it disagreed over the divinity of Christ. The Orthodox Church divided from the Roman Catholic Church over whether the Holy Spirit proceeded from the Father and the Son, or from the Father alone as declared in the Nicene Creed. Behind the division was the question of who had the authority to change the creed.[82]

In the Church today, there are many issues about which Christians profoundly disagree: infant baptism, women's ministry, forms of worship, issues of sexuality and more. Why didn't Jesus tell the Church in advance? The short answer is that I do not know. But it struck me that perhaps it was because the way in which the disciples treated each other when they disagreed was more important than getting the right answer.

Jesus said:

> "If you love those who love you, what credit is that to you? For even sinners love those who love them. If you do good to those who do good to you, what credit is that to you? For even sinners do the same."
>
> Luke 6:32,33

If we only get on with and love those we agree with, how are we different from members of a golf club?

In parts of the following chapters, I address some issues that I am passionate about, where there is disagreement. It would have been much easier if Jesus had just given the answers in black and white. Instead I will relate more of my journey and my struggle.

PART 4

Divisive Questions

CHAPTER 12

Who Goes to Heaven?

Earlier I quoted the beginning of the Athanasian Creed:

> WHOSOEVER will be saved: before all things it is necessary that he hold the Catholick Faith. Which Faith except every one do keep whole and undefiled: without doubt he shall perish everlastingly.

The creed reflects the traditional Christian teaching that it is Christians who go to heaven and everyone else goes to hell. This has been called an "exclusive" doctrine of salvation. As I write, I feel uncomfortable.

I remember as a teenager thinking this sounded unfair—what about the people who lived in South America before Christopher Columbus "discovered" it? What about the people of South America who rejected Christianity because of their encounter with so-called Christian Europeans who took their lands and killed them if they resisted?

What about children, dying before they have a chance to understand the gospel? What about those brought up with another faith? What about those whose experience of Christian teaching came from people who abused them?

As a friend said when reading a draft of this chapter:

> I cannot believe that someone who has not heard the Gospel risks eternal damnation from the God in whom I believe.

What does the Bible say?

However, this exclusive doctrine has been widely held in the evangelical side of the Church I grew up in and is supported by a number of verses from the New Testament.

According to John 3:16, Jesus said:

> For God so loved the world that he gave his only Son, so that everyone who believes in him may not perish but may have eternal life.

By implication this verse suggests that those who don't believe in him will perish.

In Acts, Peter said to the Jewish leaders who had conspired to kill Jesus:

> There is salvation in no one else, for there is no other name under heaven given among mortals by which we must be saved.
>
> *Acts 4:12*

And Paul, writing to the Romans, declares:

> For, "Everyone who calls on the name of the Lord shall be saved." But how are they to call on one in whom they have not believed? And how are they to believe in one of whom they have never heard? And how are they to hear without someone to proclaim him? And how are they to proclaim him unless they are sent?
>
> *Romans 10:13–15*

The doctrine that only Christians go to heaven also comes from Luther's Reformation understanding of Paul's statement that we are saved by faith.[83]

And using my reason, if it is not necessary to be a Christian to go to heaven, then why did Jesus have to die on the cross? And why should we share our faith and make disciples?

We therefore have a clash between an exclusive doctrine of salvation, based on these scriptures and arguments, and a more "universalist" doctrine that those who are not Christians can be saved. I can remember as a teenager being told that one preacher was "dodgy" because he was "a bit of a universalist". My perception is that this issue is still a significant source of division in the Church today. Some will reject scripture as a source of authority because it appears to portray a vindictive God who might judge people for being born in the wrong place or wrong culture.

But what else does the Bible say?

What about children?
The most frequent modification to this rather black-and-white exclusivist doctrine has come from people who insist that it does not apply to children. They argue that it would be unfair if children were excluded from heaven because they were not old enough to understand and draw on this verse from Matthew's Gospel to support their argument:

> Truly I tell you, unless you change and become like children, you will never enter the kingdom of heaven.
>
> *Matthew 18:3*

and

> Let the little children come to me, and do not stop them; for it is to such as these that the kingdom of heaven belongs.
>
> *Matthew 19:14*

Do these verses suggest an exemption for children? And if so, to what age? Rob Bell provocatively asks:

> If every new baby being born could grow up to not believe the right things and go to hell forever, then prematurely terminating a child's life anytime from conception to twelve years of age would

actually be the loving thing to do, guaranteeing that the child ends up in heaven, and not hell, forever. Why run the risk?[84]

I have to agree that an exemption only for children to an exclusive salvation theology does not stand up to logical scrutiny.

Salvation by works?
There are other parts of the Gospels which also raise questions for an over-simplified doctrine of salvation by faith alone:

- In Matthew 25:31–46, Jesus said that when the Son of Man comes in glory, he will separate people into two groups. The one group who fed the hungry, gave water to the thirsty, and welcomed strangers, etc., are the righteous. They will enter "eternal life". The other group who did not do these things are to be sent away to "eternal punishment". Those who are saved are rewarded for their actions, not their belief.
- Before Jesus told the Parable of the Good Samaritan, a lawyer asked him, "What must I do to inherit eternal life?" Jesus asked what he thought. He replied that we should, "Love the Lord your God with all your heart, and with all your soul, and with all your strength, and with all your mind; and your neighbour as yourself." Jesus replied, "Do this, and you will live" (Luke 10:25–28). Again, Jesus speaks of actions not belief.
- And in Matthew 7:21–23, Jesus said: "Not everyone who says to me, 'Lord, Lord', will enter the kingdom of heaven, but only one who does the will of my Father in heaven. On that day many will say to me, 'Lord, Lord, did we not prophesy in your name, and cast out demons in your name, and do many deeds of power in your name?' Then I will declare to them, "I never knew you; go away from me, you evildoers."

Given that James said, "[F]aith by itself, if it has no works, is dead" (James 2:17), I do not see the above scriptures as contradicting a doctrine of salvation by faith. However, it is odd, if we want to hold to a doctrine of salvation by faith alone, that the above quotations make no mention of faith.

What about Moses and Elijah?
A significant biblical contradiction to the salvation by Christian faith alone argument comes from Jesus on the Mount of Transfiguration. When Jesus was transfigured, he spoke with Moses and Elijah (Matthew 17:1–8). Neither Moses nor Elijah knew about Jesus' death and resurrection, and yet they are shown as alive and well, talking with Jesus. How could they have faith in Jesus when they did not know the story? How could they be saved by his name, when they did not know it?

Paul's story
I think that to understand Paul's teaching on salvation by faith, it is important to remember his context. Paul had been a Pharisee, fastidious in following the law before his conversion. His zeal for his faith led to his involvement in the murder of Stephen, and the persecution of the Early Church. Then on the road to Damascus he encountered Jesus and realized how wrong he had been. At the point where he knew that he deserved death for what he had done wrong, he received forgiveness. He was on a journey to Damascus to try to arrest Ananias, and yet Ananias came to him and brought healing. Paul knew that he deserved to be rejected, to die for his crimes, and yet he found forgiveness and love. I think that sums up Paul's teaching. He could do nothing to earn his forgiveness. It came as a wonderful free gift. His theology is derived from his knowledge of Jesus, his experience of forgiveness and his reason.

The apostle Peter could tell a similar story. Before Jesus was arrested, Peter had declared that even if everyone else deserted, he would stand by Jesus. But Jesus said that before the cock crowed, Peter would deny him three times. After Jesus was arrested Peter's nerve failed. Three times Peter denied that he even knew Jesus. When he realized what he had done, he wept. When Jesus rose again Peter must have been delighted, but I expect he also felt that he was a failure, even a laughing stock. But three times Jesus asked him, "Do you love me?" Three times Peter replied, "Yes Lord, you know that I love you." Three times, Jesus reinstated Peter as a shepherd, even the chief shepherd: "Feed my lambs . . . Tend my sheep . . .

Feed my sheep" (John 21:15-17). As I have said in sermons, Jesus asked Peter three times, not to rub it in but to rub it out.

So, I can passionately declare that I believe that, like Peter and Paul, none of us deserve to become God's children. None of us deserve to go to heaven. We receive God's wonderful gift as a child receives a parent's love before they can give anything back. We can receive God's wonderful gift even when, unlike children, we have behaved abominably. We are saved by grace, by God's extraordinary generosity. I think that that is what Paul meant by salvation by faith, as opposed to salvation by works.

We are saved by God, by his generosity, revealed on the cross. Knowledge of God's love in this life means we can know and experience that forgiveness now. But that does not mean that a lack of knowledge in this life must damn us for eternity.

The authority of the breadth of the Bible
In the above arguments, I have attempted to explain why I cannot agree with an exclusive "only Christians go to heaven" doctrine. The arguments against such a doctrine, using reason, are obvious: why should God reject people purely because they have not had the opportunity to hear the gospel? At first this seemed in conflict with biblical teaching, but looking at a broader range of biblical texts reveals a different picture. Moses and Elijah appear on the Mount of Transfiguration, but in their earthly lives they did not know the facts of Jesus' life or even his name.

Therefore I do not believe that we have to choose between accepting the authority of biblical revelation and the authority of reason. Instead, if we are to arrive at a doctrine of salvation that includes the breadth of the verses mentioned in this chapter we need to use our reason. If we have the humility to believe that our reason might be wrong, then we need to state any conclusions with caution. Going back to my engineer's principles, there are some things I would stake my life on, and there are other issues which are much more open to question.

My conclusion is that all the texts point to the belief that we cannot save ourselves, and that we cannot earn our place in heaven. We are saved, we can become God's children, only because of God's extraordinary generosity. The instance of Moses and Elijah on the Mount of Transfiguration shows that God's generosity is not constrained by our ignorance. I do not believe that we can say any more for certain concerning how God will deal with those who do not get the opportunity to know that good news.

Going back to my conclusions in chapter 7, I do not believe that Jesus' death on the cross enabled God to forgive us. God is by nature a forgiving God. However, in this life we can only know that good news through knowledge of Jesus and what he did for us. It is the cross that breaks the chains of our guilt and fear.

Luther taught a doctrine of "*sola scriptura*"; the idea that scripture is the only source of authority. However, Luther also taught that the Epistle of James was an "epistle of straw". Luther rejected James, which is part of the New Testament, because it didn't agree with his interpretation of the rest of the New Testament. I think we need to have the humility to admit that our interpretation might be flawed, and to always look to the full breadth of scripture.

So do we need to share the good news?

At the beginning of this section I quoted Paul writing:

> For, 'Everyone who calls on the name of the Lord shall be saved.' But how are they to call on one in whom they have not believed? And how are they to believe in one of whom they have never heard? And how are they to hear without someone to proclaim him? And how are they to proclaim him unless they are sent?
>
> Romans 10:13-15

I then made arguments that mean that if we fail to share the good news with people in this life it might not matter, because God could have other ways of saving them. If this is the case, one might ask, why bother to share the good news in the first place? Was Paul wrong in the above verses?

This criticism of universalism has force if the only reason for sharing our faith was so that people might go to heaven. I have certainly heard preachers saying that that was the main reason for sharing our faith. As

I have reflected, it strikes me that if that is all that our faith is about, it is rather sad.

Mary Magdalene, Paul, Peter, Zacchaeus and so many others found God's salvation when they encountered Jesus on earth. Their lives were transformed. Salvation was not just about going to heaven when they died, it transformed their life there and then. Me too.

It is in Jesus' life, and in his death on the cross, that God's character is truly revealed. It is Jesus' death on the cross that shows up the evil of the world and gives us a model for defeating it.

Right now, God loves us as a perfect father and wants to adopt us as his children. Why should people have to wait because we could not be bothered to tell them the news?

Christianity is not just about what I might get out of my faith. Being God's children should involve loving people now. God loved the world so much he sent Jesus into the world. If we are to follow his example, and grow his kingdom, then that involves bringing his kingdom into the world now, not just waiting to die and go to heaven.

So yes, we do need to share the good news, so that people can know they are adopted as God's children. We need to share our faith, so that they can know the hope of eternal life, and so that in response they can join in with continuing what Jesus began. Growing God's kingdom is not just about sending people to heaven. Knowing God's love, and his promise of eternal life, makes a difference to my life now.

Does God really send people to hell?

The other side of the question of who goes to heaven, is whether God really does send people to eternal punishment in hell. St Paul experienced God's forgiveness when he knew he did not deserve it. Paul had colluded in murder, but instead received God's forgiveness. Does that apply to everyone? Do all receive God's forgiveness?

Traditional Christian teaching has been definite that some are destined for hell, unless they repent. Dante's *Inferno* describes nine circles of hell with those who commit treachery in the centre. Looking at some of the evils of history and more recent times leads to the natural conclusion that some, like Hitler, must be in hell, if God is a God of justice.

But what does the Bible actually say?

Jesus' teaching on judgement
Jesus speaks quite specifically about judgement being like:

- people missing out on a wedding feast, because they turned down the invitation or were not ready (Matthew 22:1-14; Luke 14:15-24; Matthew 25:1-13)
- weeds that grew amongst the wheat being burned at harvest (Matthew 13:18-23)
- servants who are rewarded or punished depending on whether they have used the master's resources well, or were ready for when he returned (Matthew 25:14-30; Luke 19:11-27; Luke 12:35-48)
- judgement for a debtor who received mercy but then did not show that mercy to another (Matthew 18:21-35).

So Jesus does speak explicitly about judgement. Our reason, looking at the evils of world history, demands judgement. The question that has caused debate is the form of that judgement.

In the Gospels Jesus uses the word "Gehenna" eleven times. This word is often translated as hell. Rob Bell, in his book *Love Wins*, points out that Gehenna was a valley just outside Jerusalem which was used as a rubbish dump. It was seen as a cursed valley, following the child sacrifices to the god Molech that had taken place there (Jeremiah 7:31,32). It had been a burial ground, and had fires that did not go out, and wild dogs that gnashed their teeth. The word had then come to have the additional meaning of hell in Jewish culture. So Jesus said:

> If your right eye causes you to sin, tear it out and throw it away; it is better for you to lose one of your members than for your whole body to be thrown into hell [Greek: Gehenna].
>
> *Matthew 5:29*

Rob Bell suggests that Jesus might have meant that it was better to truly repent of sin rather than experience hell on earth, or to be buried in Gehenna. Rob Bell is quite graphic in his descriptions of his experience of "hell on earth".[85]

However, I do not think that Jesus can have meant purely death, or "hell on earth", when he used the word Gehenna. In Matthew 10:28 Jesus says:

> Do not fear those who kill the body but cannot kill the soul; rather fear him who can destroy both soul and body in hell [Gehenna].

And in Luke 12:5:

> But I will warn you whom to fear: fear him who, after he has killed, has authority to cast into hell. Yes, I tell you, fear him!

From these verses it seems to me to be clear that Jesus is speaking about somewhere we might go after we die.

Eternal punishment?

Jesus seems to speak of eternal punishment in the Parable of the Sheep and the Goats Jesus states that at the end of the age, there will be judgement. Those who have fed the hungry, etc, will "inherit the kingdom". In contrast, those who have failed to feed the hungry will:

> [G]o away into eternal punishment.
>
> *Matthew 25:46*

The phrase "eternal punishment" seems like a conclusive argument for Jesus believing in eternal punishment in hell. However, Rob Bell points out that the Greek is open to interpretation.[86] His argument illustrates the need for us to be cautious in our interpretation of scripture, when Jesus spoke Aramaic, which was translated into Greek, and into English for our benefit.

The phrase "eternal punishment" is a translation of "*kolasin aionion*". *Aionion* is the adjective form of *aion*, and *aion* can mean eternal or it can mean an age. For example, in Matthew 13:39, Jesus said "the harvest is the end of the age". The word translated "age" is "*aion*". As it has an end it is not eternal in this context. So could "a*ionion*" mean "for a long time" instead of "eternal"?

According to the *Theological Dictionary of the New Testament*,[87] the adjectival form, "*aionion*", always means eternal in every other instance it is used in the New Testament. But Bell's argument is still a reminder of the uncertainty inherent in some translating.

The Greek word translated as "punishment" is "*kolasin*", which the *Theological Dictionary of the New Testament* states could also mean "to lop" or "cut short". Rob Bell states that it is used elsewhere in Greek literature as a horticultural term.

As such Bell states that the wicked could go away for "an age of pruning" rather than eternal punishment. He supports this argument by referring to verses such as Philippians 2:10,11:

> [A]t the name of Jesus every knee should bend, in heaven and on earth and under the earth, and every tongue should confess that Jesus Christ is Lord, to the glory of God the Father.

If one day "every knee will bend and every tongue confess", should that not include the "wicked"?[88]

The Parable of the Rich Man and Lazarus also portrays hell as involving eternal torment (Luke 16:19–31). The rich man who ignores the plight of Lazarus, the beggar at his gate, ends up going to Hades:

> [W]here he was being tormented, he looked up and saw Abraham far away with Lazarus by his side.

Again, this seems to indicate eternal punishment, with no possibility of escape, but, as Bell points out, it is a parable. Parables are teaching stories, which are not to be taken as literal truth.

Annihilation?

In contrast to the image of eternal torment, Revelation 20:13–15 says:

> [A]ll were judged according to what they had done. Then Death and Hades were thrown into the lake of fire. This is the second death, the lake of fire; and anyone whose name was not found written in the book of life was thrown into the lake of fire.

These verses do speak specifically about judgement, though Revelation is of course open to varying interpretations. The significant point about this passage, as we consider whether hell might involve eternal punishment, is that the passage appears to speak about annihilation. As G. B. Caird says in his commentary:

> If we protest that we cannot accommodate our minds to the idea of eternal torment, the answer is that neither could John. He believed that, if at the end there should be any who remained impervious to the grace and love of God, they would be thrown, with Death and Hades, into the lake of fire which is the second death, i.e. extinction and total oblivion.[89]

John Stott also argued for annihilation, rather than eternal torment, based primarily on this passage from Revelation, and Jesus' words in Matthew 10:28, that we should fear him who can destroy both body *and soul* in hell.[90]

In reading John Stott's argument, I was particularly struck by these words:

> Will the final destiny of the impertinent be eternal conscious torment, "for ever and ever", or will it be total annihilation of their being? The former has to be described as traditional orthodoxy... Emotionally I find the concept intolerable... But our emotions are a fluctuating, unreliable guide to the truth and must not be exalted to the place of supreme authority... My question must be—and is—not what does my heart tell me, but

what does God's word say? And in order to answer this question, we need to survey the biblical material afresh and to open our minds (not just our hearts) to the possibility that scripture points in the direction of annihilation.[91]

Conclusion

Going back to my four sources for theology, in this chapter I have used the mixture of revelation, reason, experience and other people to consider the questions of who goes to heaven and whether people go to hell. At first it felt to me that the sources of revelation and reason were pulling in opposite directions. It felt that they were incompatible.

However, I now feel that by using a wider range of Bible passages, my approach of combining the sources of reason and scripture is justified. I still believe that God's revelation in scripture must be our primary source of authority. Our reason, and our emotions, may be flawed. However, we have to use our reason in our interpretation of scripture.

I am happy to trust that Jesus offers me eternal life, and that by turning to him and trusting him I can be a child of God. I do not deserve it. That gift comes from God's extraordinary generosity. This good news is revealed in how Jesus treated people, in the cross, and in the lives of Peter and Paul. That is amazing good news, and something to be shared.

I do not think that God has revealed to us through the Bible exactly how he will treat those who in this life do not know him, or reject him, but I do believe that there will be judgement in some form. The Bible warns us of it, and my reason demands it. But I also believe that God's mercy and love is beyond our understanding.

CHAPTER 13

Sexuality and a Divided Church

When I was planning to write this book, my intention was always that the last chapters were to be about how we respond to theology. In the following chapters I am writing about some practical global issues that are relevant to theology, and which I care about. But the first of these issues, sexuality, is difficult. The questions are very personal and raise great passions. However, I feel I need to write about homosexuality because of how the lesbian and gay community have been treated in the past and because the issue has divided the Church of England, and much of the worldwide Church. Jesus did not duck difficult questions, although sometimes he asked further questions instead of giving answers.

In this chapter I will explain how my understanding has developed, using my model of mixed sources for theology, as described in chapter 3. I hope that telling my story, incorporating the different sources, might help all the Church move forward, and that it might also be a model for approaching other issues that divide the Church that I have not addressed in this book.

My first thoughts: Hypocrisy

I was exposed to questions concerning homosexuality for the first time when I was nineteen, at university. We had a meeting between members of the Christian Union, the Chaplaincy and members of the university's LGBT society.

I came away from that meeting feeling angry at the awful hypocrisy of the Church. Jesus said:

> Why do you see the speck in your neighbour's eye, but do not notice the log in your own eye? Or how can you say to your neighbour, "Let me take the speck out of your eye", while the log is in your own eye? You hypocrite, first take the log out of your own eye, and then you will see clearly to take the speck out of your neighbour's eye.
>
> *Matthew 7:3–5*

The Church has so often been silent on the issue of money, and yet Jesus spoke more about wealth than any other issue. Wealth is considered a private issue, but we can see the sizes of each other's houses, the cars we drive, and we do not tend to be secretive about where we go on holiday. We have Jesus' command to love our neighbours, and we have poverty displayed on our TVs. Is wealth really a private matter? As a vicar I know that the Church is so often short of money for good projects. But we feel people should be free to make their own decisions about their money without being judged.

In contrast, the Church has condemned and, in the past, made illegal private acts between two consenting adults. The prosecution and subsequent chemical castration of Alan Turing, as shown in the film *The Imitation Game*, is an awful example, but only the tip of the iceberg.

What makes this hypocrisy even more abhorrent is our attitude to adultery, which is forbidden in the Ten Commandments. It has been frowned upon but without any criminal sanctions. There have been an extraordinary number of known mistresses to our British kings who are called "Defenders of the Faith" at their coronation.

Or we pray " . . . forgive us our sins as we forgive those who sin against us", and yet in every church I have been a minister in I have had people telling me about grievances going back years. All too often those grievances are just accepted.

I hope that the whole Church would agree that we must condemn this hypocrisy. We cannot condone making an issue out of homosexual practice, which is not a temptation to the majority, while ignoring the sins that are well known and explicitly condemned by Jesus.

My second thought: Sympathy

My second thought from that first meeting was one of strong sympathy with those who were gay. It did seem unfair that the Bible, as I understood it, declared homosexual actions to be sinful.

I have since heard a number of those who were gay stating that they would not want to have anything to do with God if he rejected them for who they were. The response that God loves them, but hates homosexual practice, was no help.

As I sympathize with those who reject God because of the suffering they see and experience, so I sympathize with those who reject God because of their understanding, or the Church's understanding, of God's attitude to homosexuality.

My third thought: We cannot pick and choose—God knows best

For all the sympathy and anger at hypocrisy, I was still left with my understanding of what the Bible says.

In the Old Testament most explicitly we have:

> You shall not lie with a male as with a woman; it is an abomination.
> *Leviticus 18:22*

and

> If a man lies with a male as with a woman, both of them have committed an abomination; they shall be put to death; their blood is upon them.
> *Leviticus 20:13*

Then Paul writes:

> [M]en, giving up natural intercourse with women, were consumed with passion for one another. Men committed shameless acts with

men and received in their own persons the due penalty for their error.

Romans 1:27,28

Do you not know that wrongdoers will not inherit the kingdom of God? Do not be deceived! Fornicators, idolaters, adulterers, male prostitutes, sodomites, thieves, the greedy, drunkards, revilers, robbers—none of these will inherit the kingdom of God. And this is what some of you used to be. But you were washed, you were sanctified, you were justified in the name of the Lord Jesus Christ and in the Spirit of our God.

1 Corinthians 6:9–11

It should be noted that there has been some debate as to the correct translation of the word rendered by the NRSV as "sodomites". Reading the story of Sodom and Gomorrah the people were intent on rape. To equate a loving consensual relationship between two people of the same sex with the actions of Sodom and Gomorrah is offensive. However, from the above it is clear that Leviticus condemns male homosexual practice in the strongest possible terms, and that Paul considers such acts as sinful.

My upbringing, considering the Bible as the word of God, meant that I felt that I could not just pick and choose the bits of the Bible that I agreed with. I hated the hypocrisy of the Church, and I had sympathy with those who might reject God because of what the Bible said about homosexuality. However, I was not prepared to take the step of saying that my reasoning must be right and God or Leviticus or Paul "must be wrong".

But what about the rest of the Bible?

The above quotations are only a few verses out of the whole Bible. Some of the complexity of the Bible was wonderfully illustrated in the American political drama, *The West Wing*. In one episode a talk show host defends calling homosexuality an "abomination" by saying that that is what the Bible says in Leviticus 18:22, as quoted above.

President Bartlett responded by saying that he was interested in selling his youngest daughter into slavery, as allowed by Exodus 21:7. He asked what a good price would be. He said that his chief of staff, insisted on working on the Sabbath, and that Exodus 35:2 states that that means he should be killed. Bartlett asked whether he could ask the police to do it. He then noted that Leviticus 11:7 states that we can't touch dead pig skins. He asked whether American footballers could continue to handle balls made of pig skin leather if they wore gloves?[92]

If we look at the whole of Leviticus rather than just a couple of verses, we will discover the disturbing truth that the Old Testament law demands the death penalty for all sorts of actions that we routinely practice.

In *The West Wing*, the talk show host makes no reply, and sadly that then brands all those who believe that the Bible condemns homosexual practice as hypocrites and bigots. Reading the book of Acts does give another side to the story.

The New Testament church and its attitude to the law

I wrote in chapter 10 that if I was Jesus, I would have given the disciples a very detailed list of instructions about how they were to behave and how they were to continue the mission Jesus began. It would have saved a lot of arguments, but Jesus didn't. Instead he said that the Spirit would lead them into all truth. In Acts 10, the Holy Spirit began showing the disciples that they should set aside significant parts of the Old Testament law. But the Spirit didn't tell the whole church at the same time. He just told Peter. Not surprisingly, arguments followed. In Acts 15, they listened to one another, combining scripture with Peter and Paul's experiences. The conclusion they came to was put in a letter to the Gentiles:

> For it has seemed good to the Holy Spirit and to us to impose on you no further burden than these essentials: that you abstain from what has been sacrificed to idols and from blood and from what is strangled and from fornication.
>
> *Acts 15:28,29*

I wrote that Acts 15 gives a good model for listening, combining scripture, reason, experience and their understanding of God's revelation through the Holy Spirit. What was more uncomfortable was that God's revelation to Peter, and their combined experience and reason, in the end overcame their understanding of God's commands in the Old Testament. Might that mean that the Spirit today could be leading the Church into changing its attitude to homosexuality?

In the above quotation, the disciples wrote that the Gentiles should abstain from fornication, or in other translations sexual immorality. The Church would have understood this as meaning that the sexual prohibitions of the Old Testament law should remain. That interpretation is then reflected in Paul's writing.

If we consider the declaration of Acts 15 binding for all time, then we can lay aside all the Old Testament law, apart from these prohibitions against eating food sacrificed to idols, blood and sexual immorality. In theory the talk show host in *The West Wing* could have given this as an answer.

However, if we were to abide by Acts 15, we would have to stop eating black pudding which is made from blood, and we should drain blood from all animals before eating them, as both Muslims and Jews still do. The reason that the Church now has no prohibitions concerning eating blood, is that we now understand that Jesus was hinting that we could eat anything. Mark 7:14–19 says:

> "Listen to me, all of you, and understand: there is nothing outside a person that by going in can defile, but the things that come out are what defile . . . Whatever goes into a person from outside cannot defile, since it enters not the heart but the stomach, and goes out into the sewer." (Thus he declared all foods clean.)

The comment, "Thus he declared all foods clean", was added by the Early Church. They were not Jesus' words.

Acts 15 is not binding concerning eating blood. It was a ruling given for a particular time and place, which we can now disregard. If the ruling concerning eating blood is not binding for us, what about Acts 15's instruction on Old Testament sexual prohibitions?

In Chapter 10 I argued that the Spirit continued to lead the Church into truth after the New Testament was written, in particular concerning slavery. Paul wrote that masters should treat their slaves well, but he never said that slavery was an abomination that should be abolished. Jesus gave a strong hint about abolishing slavery when he said that he had come to set the captives free (Luke 4:18). Paul didn't fully get the hint, but took a step in the right direction.

So Acts 15's ruling, concerning eating blood, and Paul's attitude to slavery, are now considered a step in the right direction, but fell short of where the Spirit was leading. Jesus hinted at the changes, but left the Spirit to lead the Church into truth.

Did Jesus give any hints about changing our attitudes to homosexuality? A colleague commented:

> Jesus never mentioned the issue? What does that clue say about our obsession with it?

Richard Burridge in his book *Imitating Jesus*[93] goes further in arguing that Jesus created an inclusive community, and that we should follow his example. Concerning Paul's words on homosexuality, Burridge describes them as a "work in progress", perhaps like the instruction of Acts 15 and Paul's teaching on slavery. Paul would not have known of the committed life-long same sex relationships that are a feature of our discussions today.

You will know them by their fruit

So if we admit the possibility that the Holy Spirit might be leading the Church to change its attitude to homosexuality, how do we know? Paul wrote:

> Do not despise the words of prophets, but test everything; hold fast to what is good; abstain from every form of evil.
>
> *1 Thessalonians 5:20–22*

But how do we test? If part of the Church thinks that the Spirit is leading in one direction and another part disagrees, how do we move forward? Jesus said:

> "Beware of false prophets, who come to you in sheep's clothing but inwardly are ravenous wolves. You will know them by their fruits. Are grapes gathered from thorns, or figs from thistles? In the same way, every good tree bears good fruit, but the bad tree bears bad fruit. A good tree cannot bear bad fruit, nor can a bad tree bear good fruit. Every tree that does not bear good fruit is cut down and thrown into the fire. Thus you will know them by their fruits."
>
> *Matthew 7:15–20*

The Early Church could see the fruit of Peter and Paul's ministry amongst the Gentiles so they came to accept it, and accept the radical change in the law.

I have known a number of people who were initially opposed to the ordination of women, who changed their minds when they saw the good fruit in the lives and ministries of women priests. I also know people who have changed their minds about the ministry of those who are gay, and the faith of those who are gay, when they have got to know them.

I can see both sides of the argument, and I pray that the Spirit will lead us into truth. I have changed my mind.

Why didn't Jesus tell them in advance?

In chapter 10, I asked "Why didn't Jesus tell them in advance". Pertinent to this chapter, why did he not make clear how his followers should conduct their intimate personal lives? As I wrote, perhaps it was because the way in which the disciples treated each other when they disagreed was more important than getting the right answer:

> "If you love those who love you, what credit is that to you? For even sinners love those who love them. If you do good to those

> who do good to you, what credit is that to you? For even sinners do the same."
>
> *Luke 6:32,33*

Going back to my engineering analogy of tolerance, I hope that all Christians will condemn the hypocrisy of making an issue about homosexuality while ignoring actions that Jesus specifically condemns. I hope that all would share my sympathy for the experience of gay people, and my feeling that the commands of Leviticus seem to lack justification. I hope also that all could understand and have sympathy with those who stick to the traditional restrictions on sex, because of their humility in submitting to the Bible as the inspired word of God. I hope that this "tolerance" might be a foundation for bringing God's light and healing into the world, even when we disagree.

New Covenant not Old Covenant

The Bible starts with accounts of the creation and the fall. I don't believe these accounts are meant to be literal history, but that they contain profound truth about how the world is now. In particular the accounts of the fall strike me as significant insights into the way evil continues to come into our world today.

In Genesis 3, Adam and Eve eat the forbidden fruit. Adam and Eve are depicted in paradise, having everything they could want, but are told they must not eat fruit from just one tree: the tree of the knowledge of good and evil. And they break the only rule they have been given.

I find it fascinating and horrifying that Adam and Eve reject the one rule they know for certain, in order to have access to knowledge of good and evil. Do Christians sometimes do the same? We ignore the command of Jesus that we know for certain, that we should love our neighbours, including our enemies. Instead we have been angry and at times violent with those we disagree with in much more debatable matters. We love to judge, ignoring or hiding our own shortcomings.

And so today, when it comes to our debates about how we worship, whether women can be priests or bishops, and whether homosexual acts are sinful, we seem determined to judge each other, to define what is right and what is wrong. In areas where we have legitimate reasons to disagree, we condemn each other, all too often ignoring the one command we know for certain that Jesus said: Love.

PART 5

Faith in Action

CHAPTER 14

Faith without Works is Dead: Growing the Kingdom of God

Engineers are concerned with putting theory into practice in the real world. James states:

> What good is it, my brothers and sisters, if you say you have faith but do not have works? Can faith save you? If a brother or sister is naked and lacks daily food, and one of you says to them, 'Go in peace; keep warm and eat your fill', and yet you do not supply their bodily needs, what is the good of that? So faith by itself, if it has no works, is dead.
>
> James 2:14–17

My final chapters concern how should we, as Christians, respond to our theology?

Faith is not just about belief. As many preachers have said, the great tightrope walker Blondin pushed a wheelbarrow over a rope suspended across the Niagara Falls. He asked the applauding crowd if they thought he could do it again, and they all said yes. He asked if any would like to sit in the wheelbarrow as he did it, and no one volunteered. Real faith leads to action.

More than a 'to do' list

Jesus' first command to his disciples was to follow him. Going through the Gospels could give a list of tasks that are part of that call:

love God with all our heart, soul, mind and strength (Matthew 22:37, 38; Luke 10:27);

love our neighbours, including our enemies (Matthew 5:44–46; 7:12; 22:39; Luke 10:27);

make disciples (Matthew 28:19, 20);

let children come to Jesus (Matthew 19:14);

be peacemakers (Matthew 5:9);

be light and salt in the world (Matthew 5:13–16);

do not judge (Matthew 7:1–5);

do not lust (Matthew 5:28–30);

deny ourselves and take up our crosses (Luke 9:23–25);

be servants (Matthew 20:26–28; John 13:12–17);

heal the sick (Matthew 10:8).

But Jesus did not give the disciples a new book of Leviticus. He didn't come to give a "to do" list. Following him is much more radical.

Being disciples and God's adopted children

When Jesus called Andrew, Peter, James and John to follow him (Matthew 4:18–22), they left their work as fishermen and became his disciples. A disciple was not just an apprentice, learning to do what a master did, like learning a trade. A disciple also aimed to be like their master, to take on their character. The heart of our response to our theology must be to be disciples, to continue the work he began, and to be like him. He had a radical way of changing the world. We are called to imitate him.

Jesus was different from every other rabbi as he is God the Son. Being like him means being God's adopted children. Putting our faith into practice starts with being disciples, God's children, rather than a "to do" list. That is the foundation for action.

Jesus' relationship with his Father was realized through his prayer life. Jesus frequently got up early or stayed up at night to pray (e.g. Matthew 14:23, 26:31–44; Mark 1:35, 6:46). My personal relationship with God started when I tried praying.

For us to be children of God, we also need to pray. To go into detail would require another book, but one talk I heard when I was a teenager is significant: Often we think of prayer as trying to get God to do what we want, but actually prayer is about us changing so that we want what God wants. When we pray, "your kingdom come, your will be done", we cannot really mean it unless we are willing to change ourselves.

This links to the theology of the previous chapters. If I was God, I would have changed the world using thunderbolts, but Jesus came to change the world in a radically different way. Being a disciple means changing to be like Jesus.

In the following pages, I will not address all the individual commands from the Gospels, but the subjects I have chosen are ones that seem to illustrate the principles of how we can continue to do what Jesus did, and imitate him.

Making disciples in unexpected ways

In Jesus' call to those fishermen who became his first disciples he promised that he would make them fishers of people. He repeated that call, in different language, before he physically left them:

> "Go therefore and make disciples of all nations, baptizing them in the name of the Father and of the Son and of the Holy Spirit, and teaching them to obey everything that I have commanded you."
> *Matthew 28:19–20*

We are called not just to be disciples, but also to make disciples. We are called not just to be God's adopted children, but also to invite and welcome others into the family, as Jesus did. But how?

Jesus and those first disciples taught publicly in the synagogues, by the lake shore and in the public meeting places. It is easy to think of making disciples in that context, and as a vicar that is what I try to do with my preaching and teaching.

However, looking at Jesus in action, and at my own journey of faith, suggests that becoming a disciple is a much richer process than merely listening to a sermon and deciding to agree with it.

Jesus told the parable of the sower who sowed seed everywhere, some on paths, some on shallow soil, some amongst weeds and some on good soil. It was only the seed on the good soil that produced a crop (Matthew 13:1–8).

Looking at the Gospels and the Early Church reveals that good soil was found in unlikely places. Jesus did not pick the religious or educational elite as his first disciples. He picked four fishermen, two of whom were known for their foul tempers, and another one who consistently got things wrong and let Jesus down. He included a tax collector and a zealot, a bit like picking Margaret Thatcher and Arthur Scargill, or Donald Trump and Hillary Clinton, for the same team.

The extraordinary nature of Jesus' call to discipleship is that the most unlikely candidates were transformed. The heart of the Gospel is God's adoption of us as his children. We don't deserve it, but it comes as a wonderful free gift. As part of the package, God can transform any of us, and so our calling to make disciples involves inviting everyone, however unpromising.

Jesus' methods are illustrated in his call to Zacchaeus. Zacchaeus was rejected by his community as a sinner, but Jesus ate with him without a word of condemnation. It was that radical, counter-cultural love that prepared the soil, and led to the change.

In contrast, I can think of many others who have been turned off church by their experience. In the wonderful novel *The Ragged Trousered Philanthropists*,[94] the members of the church are shown to be extraordinarily hypocritical. The church used so-called charity as a tool for control and subjugation of the ordinary hard-working members of the community. The church in the novel hardened the soil, so that the gospel never took root.

Jesus also spoke of the kingdom of God being like a mustard seed that grows from apparent insignificance into a great shrub. I wrote about that being a metaphor for Jesus' ministry, starting so small and now touching every nation on earth. It strikes me that it can also describe how apparently insignificant actions can have lifelong consequences in the area of discipleship.

In my engineering research into metal fatigue, even small defects could have catastrophic consequences. Equally it only takes one spark to start an explosion. The horticultural analogy is a much more positive example of the extra consequences of small actions.

For example, when I was six years old, my family moved to Birmingham and started attending our local church. Miss Fowler seemed quite old to me then and was the last person in the church to be known by her Christian name, but she played a crucial part in welcoming us into the family service. She asked whether my older sister and brother and then I would like to read the readings or the prayers in the service. She faithfully sorted out rotas and made sure we rehearsed, so that everyone could hear us. A small action, along with many other small actions, that changed my life.

The above is primarily about how I and others started our journey of faith. However, Jesus also shows that we are not transformed in an instant, and that growing disciples takes a long-term commitment. I think of Jesus, challenging and rebuking Peter when he got things wrong, but always in the context that he was loved.

When I was a teenager, I had a relationship with God, but I had rebelled. I lived a double life, going to church on Sundays and in the week going to punk rock concerts and drinking and smoking underage. Then, when I was sixteen, my closest friend went to Australia. Finding myself short of friends, I went back to the school Christian Union that I had attended when I was younger. I found a level of friendship, acceptance and honesty there that opened me up to renew my discipleship. It was that honesty and friendship that enabled me to talk through questions I have struggled with, address attitudes that were quite unchristian, and continue my journey.

Being a disciple means imitating Jesus. Making disciples means imitating how Jesus prepared the soil, sowed seed and nurtured faith.

Refined by fire and water

In engineering terms, the Old Testament prophets speak of God refining or purifying his people with fire, and that affliction can function like purifying fire. Gold and silver are purified by heating to melting point, so that dross rises to the surface and can be skimmed off:

> And I will put this third into the fire, refine them as
>   one refines silver, and test them as gold is tested.
> They will call on my name, and I will answer them.
>
> *Zechariah 13:9*

> See, I have refined you, but not like silver;
> I have tested you in the furnace of adversity.
>
> *Isaiah 48:10*

John the Baptist described Jesus as being greater than him because John baptized with just water, while Jesus would baptize with the Holy Spirit and fire (Matthew 3:11). The water probably reflects a more superficial cleansing while the fire speaks of a more radical transformation. The snippets we see of the lives of some of the early disciples involve them being transformed, often in uncomfortable ways:

- Peter's overconfidence was shown up when he promised that he was willing to die for Jesus, and lost his nerve. Three times he denied even knowing Jesus. But then after the resurrection, Jesus reinstated Peter as a shepherd of his people by asking three times whether he loved him (John 21:15–19).
- Paul's ignorant persecuting zeal was corrected on the road to Damascus, with Paul being blinded, before being healed by those he was planning to persecute (Acts 9:1–19).

Perhaps reflecting on his life, Paul wrote:

> [W]e also boast in our sufferings, knowing that suffering produces endurance, and endurance produces character, and character produces hope ...
>
> *Romans 5:3,4*

Being a disciple means imitating Jesus. The lives of those first disciples reveal how they were changed, healed and transformed by Jesus. Suffering and failure were part of the process. I can look back at my own life and see how I have changed through failure, stress, the honesty of friends and forgiveness. Those friends were in imperfect ways imitating Jesus.

Healing

Jesus said:

> Very truly, I tell you, the one who believes in me will also do the works that I do and, in fact, will do greater works than these, because I am going to the Father.
>
> *John 14:12*

At first sight, the idea that the disciples might do greater things than Jesus did seems astonishing. One obvious interpretation is that we can do greater things by being numerically greater. Every Christian Aid Week Christians will raise enough money to feed millions. We can do greater things than Jesus did because there are more of us. It doesn't have to involve feeding 10,000 with just three loaves and one fish.

But just focusing on the numerical meaning of the word greater would distract from the most surprising or controversial part of Jesus' commands. Jesus told his disciples to teach the next generation, "[T]o obey everything that I have commanded you" (Matthew 28:20). And Jesus had commanded his disciples to, "Cure the sick, raise the dead, cleanse the lepers, cast out demons" (Matthew 10:8).

Jesus healed many people miraculously. In Acts we read of the disciples doing the same. As the disciples were to make disciples, teaching us to obey everything that Jesus taught, then as disciples ourselves, we also should be praying for healing.

As a child, reading the prayers in the family service, I am sure that we prayed for healing. Prayer for healing in that sense is a normal part of our worship. However, I can still remember the shock of a preacher suggesting that we might expect something to happen as we prayed, rather than healing occurring quietly at a later date.

John Wimber
When I was in my early twenties, John Wimber came to the United Kingdom and preached just that. In his book, *Power Evangelism*, he wrote that he started going to church for the first time after becoming a Christian and reading the Bible independently. He wrote that he went to his first service, joined in the singing, listened to the sermon, and then was a bit shocked when it was all over. He asked in disappointment and surprise, "Well when do we start doing it?" The other people in the church had not even thought about going into the streets and expecting the miraculous to occur.[95]

I remember my surprise when I first heard about this, and my discomfort when a preacher suggested that someone might be healed when I prayed. I could see the logic of the sermon, and its biblical basis, but it was quite outside my experience.

So, in the safe confines of the church, we "had a go". One evening I came to the church with a friend who had injured his shoulder playing basketball. At the end of the service he asked whether I might pray for his shoulder to be healed. I prayed my best prayers. I did believe that Jesus healed, and that God had healed through his first disciples. I believed he could heal through me. So I prayed, but nothing happened. I would have given up, but my friend was not content. We went to the front of the church where we told our story to someone else and they prayed. They then asked whether my friend could try lifting his arm up. He did. He could not have lifted it before the service because of the injury. I can think of three other occasions over the last thirty years where I have seen something similar:

- We had been teaching our youth group to try praying for healing, and once as part of a holiday one of them asked me to pray for her because she had an awful headache. I did not have much faith, as the last few people I had prayed for had remained sick. I did not even ask her how she felt after I prayed, and it was only later in the day when she told me that the headache had disappeared instantly.
- On two other occasions I ended up praying for people who had recently had a bad diagnosis from a doctor. On both occasions I prayed with a group for them, and nothing seemed to happen. I went away feeling mortified for them. I continued praying at length until eventually peace came. For both people I discovered afterwards that the doctors changed their diagnoses.

I could also write of numerous people that I have prayed for who have not got better. I have witnessed first-hand the horrors of some cancers, the trauma of dementia, not to mention marriages that have ended in divorce, and wars that have continued.

And yet John wrote that Jesus said to the disciples:

> I will do whatever you ask in my name, so that the Father may be glorified in the Son. If in my name you ask me for anything, I will do it.
>
> *John 14:13,14*

And James wrote:

> Are any among you sick? They should call for the elders of the church and have them pray over them, anointing them with oil in the name of the Lord. The prayer of faith will save the sick, and the Lord will raise them up; . . . . The prayer of the righteous is powerful and effective.
>
> *James 5:14–16*

I do not understand these scriptures. They are an illustration of why I thought about calling this book *An Engineer's Struggle with Theology*.

These scriptures and my experience seem to be incompatible, like the testimony and counter testimony of the Old Testament as discussed in chapter 6.

I was comforted, if that is the right word, to note Paul's throwaway comment to Timothy:

> Trophimus I left ill in Miletus.
>
> 2 Timothy 4:20

Why was Trophimus left to be ill? Didn't Paul have faith?

And Paul also writes to Timothy:

> No longer drink only water, but take a little wine for the sake of your stomach and your frequent ailments.
>
> 1 Timothy 5:23

Why did he need to take wine instead of just prayer?

I have read and heard over the years many accounts of people who have received prayer and been healed, but I have also heard the anguish of others who have received prayer with no apparent benefit.

Theologically, I do not understand, any more than I understand why God allows suffering in the first place. However, I have seen enough prayer answered in a "good" way to keep me praying. Archbishop William Temple is supposed to have said:

> When I pray, coincidences happen, and when I don't, they don't.

Theologically, I do not understand, but it does seem to fit with the parables of the kingdom of God as I explained in chapter 8. The kingdom of God is growing, but has not yet come in all its fullness. I see the answered prayer as a "first fruit", a sign of the harvest yet to come, the day when Jesus will wipe away every tear (Revelation 21:4).

I have mixed feelings concerning John Wimber's thesis that miraculous events were fundamental to God's plan for evangelism.[96] In the Gospels, Jesus often told those who had been healed not to tell anyone. Healing should not be about showing off. The crowds that followed because of the healings dispersed when he was arrested, or perhaps changed their tune to cry, "Crucify!" I do know people who have become Christians, and remained Christians, following apparently miraculous events. I find John Wimber's accounts of how the miraculous led to changed lives inspiring and challenging. I believe that healing, where it does occur, is a sign of God's love. However, given the frequent prayer that does not result in healing, testimonies of good news can give a mixed message for evangelism for those whose experience is different. But I will keep praying.

When I was about twenty-three, I went to *Spring Harvest*, a week of Christian teaching and worship based in a Butlin's holiday camp. At the beginning of the week I joined in the "prayer walk" around the camp, to pray for the week. However, partway through the walk I began to feel ill, with that awful feeling that I was going to be sick. I went back to my chalet, and told the two people I was sharing with, and then lay down in my room. Shortly afterwards they came in and offered to pray with me, as we had been taught in church. The first one prayed, and I confess that it sounded as if he, like me, had prayed for a lot of people without beneficial results. I still felt nauseous.

Then the other one started praying, and his hands shook as he put them on me. He prayed with extraordinary passion that I would not be ill, rebuking the Devil and illness and making various other theological statements that I am not sure I agree with. But as he prayed, I felt deep down that he cared for me and wanted me to have a good holiday. That prayer touched me because at the time I felt a bit of an outsider with a group who knew each other well. It brought an emotional healing that I needed. The fact that half an hour later I was sick and ended up having an early night felt insignificant in comparison. Offering to pray for someone should always come as a sign of our love, and our faith, without ever making promises or statements that are contrary to the breadth of our experience.

CHAPTER 15

Growing the Kingdom of God
Part 2: Changing the World

The kingdom of God is not just about people joining the Church, becoming children of God and worshipping him. It is also about changing the world.

Jesus declared in his first recorded sermon in Luke's Gospel:

> The Spirit of the Lord is upon me, because he has anointed me to bring good news to the poor. He has sent me to proclaim release to the captives and recovery of sight to the blind, to let the oppressed go free, to proclaim the year of the Lord's favour.
>
> *Luke 4:18,19*

He put that into practice by his preaching, by his welcome to the poor and oppressed, and by the way he led his life. He preached about what it meant to love your neighbour in the Parable of the Good Samaritan (Luke 10:25-37). He fed the hungry with five loaves and two fish. He transformed Zacchaeus (Luke 19:1-10). He also challenged and stood up to the bullying corruption of the chief priests when he turned over the tables in the temple (Matthew 21:12,13; Mark 11:15-17; Luke 19:45,46; John 2:13-16).

Money

So we also are called to change the world, if we are to be disciples. That obviously has consequences for how we use our money. Jesus spoke more about wealth than any other issue (e.g. Luke 16:1–15,19–31; Matthew 19:16–26).

In Acts 2 and Acts 4 we have a wonderful picture of the Early Church doing just that:

> All who believed were together and had all things in common; they would sell their possessions and goods and distribute the proceeds to all, as any had need.
>
> *Acts 2:44–45*

> Now the whole group of those who believed were of one heart and soul, and no one claimed private ownership of any possessions, but everything they owned was held in common.
>
> *Acts 4:32*

When I was a teenager, Ronald Sider's *Rich Christians in an Age of Hunger*[97] challenged me to put that into practice, using the parable Jesus told of the rich man and Lazarus (Luke 16:19–31). The rich man is dressed in fine linen and feasts sumptuously every day. Lazarus lay at his gate, covered with sores, and longed to eat what fell from the rich man's table. The rich man in the parable goes to hell.

Compared to so many in our world, the majority of people in the United Kingdom eat sumptuously. According to *The Guardian*, UK households threw away £13 billion worth of food in 2015.[98] According to the World Food Programme:

> In a world where we produce enough food to feed everyone, **795 million people—one in nine—still go to bed on an empty stomach each night.** Even more—one in three—suffer from some form of malnutrition.[99]

The statistics can seem so overwhelming that we think it is impossible to put things right, with the danger of us doing nothing. However, thinking of the Parable of the Mustard Seed, it is amazing to consider how our response to hunger has developed over the last seventy years.

Oxfam started during the Second World War providing relief for civilians in Greece and only responded to an emergency in a developing country when it helped India in 1951.[100] Christian Aid started as Christian Reconstruction in Europe after the Second World War and again only started looking beyond Europe in the 1950s.[101] I remember, in my childhood, Tearfund had campaigns for emergency aid following floods in Bangladesh. Tearfund only started in 1968.[102] In the 1960s Christian Aid's annual income reached £2.5 million. It had increased to £5.9 million in 1979, £28 million in 1989, and £107 million in 2015/16.[103] In addition the number of overseas aid charities has increased dramatically with the emergence of Band Aid, Live Aid, Comic Relief and Sport Relief. Because of the seeds sown by the pioneers, the aid movement has grown astonishingly. Charitable giving for those in the developing world is now mainstream and supported by countless celebrities. Like a mustard seed it has grown, with Christians playing a significant part in the process.

For this aid to continue to grow it needs us to play our part. Jesus did not give specific instructions, like a tax code. He simply commanded us to love, leaving it to the Spirit to guide us in our response.

Justice

The Early Church showed this wonderful generosity to the poor (e.g. Acts 6:1–4). However, a few years later it seems that they struggled with the problems of a "dependency culture", where widows were being added to the list and not responding in the way Paul would wish (1 Timothy 5:3–16). The worry of creating communities that are trapped by being dependent on aid has also inspired people to ask how we might be more helpful. Perhaps again the Holy Spirit is leading the Church into richer ways of responding to poverty.

Christian Aid, in particular, brought to my attention the need for long-term prosperity, with the slogan from my teenage years: "Give a man a fish and you feed him for a day, teach a man to fish and you feed him for life." In this way, Christian Aid raised the issue that what we do with our money is not just a matter of "charity" but of justice.

Isaiah 58:6,7 says:

> Is not this the fast that I choose: to loose the bonds of injustice, to undo the thongs of the yoke, to let the oppressed go free, and to break every yoke? Is it not to share your bread with the hungry, and bring the homeless poor into your house; when you see the naked, to cover them, and not to hide yourself from your own kin?

Jesus clearly saw this as part of his mission, as he declared in that first sermon:

> He has sent me to *proclaim release to the captives* and recovery of sight to the blind, *to let the oppressed go free*, to proclaim the year of the Lord's favour. [My italics]
>
> Luke 4:18,19

If we are to be imitators of Jesus, then we also have to strive for justice, and do so by following Jesus' example. I have written already about Jesus' life-changing radical love. However, he also:

> entered the temple and drove out all who were selling and buying in the temple, and he overturned the tables of the money-changers and the seats of those who sold doves. He said to them, "It is written, 'My house shall be called a house of prayer'; but you are making it a den of robbers".
>
> Matthew 21:12-13

Jesus' radical life-changing love included action, confronting the corruption of his day. So how can we set the oppressed free? One way is with the development of fair trade.

Fair trade

Traditional charity has emphasized the sharing of resources, etc., but Christian Aid and similar organizations have emphasized dealing with the causes of poverty, rather than just dealing with its symptoms. In our capitalist, free-market world, those who grow the things we eat can get paid a pittance because they have no power to dictate prices. When they go to market they have to sell, at whatever price they can get. Fairly traded products guarantee that the producers get a reasonable return for their labour. The result is that the workers can have better working conditions, education and health care for their families, and the dignity of knowing that they have provided for their families through their own work.

It is easy to think that the only way we could change unfair trade practices would be to have political power, but that is not true. When I was a teenager, I remember some Christians buying and drinking fairly traded instant coffee, because they wanted justice. I did not buy it or drink it, as it was not as nice as my normal coffee. But because of the sacrifices of those first pioneers, the fair trade movement has grown astonishingly—another mustard seed story:

> In 1997, Fairtrade International was formed, uniting many fair trade organizations under one umbrella.
>
> In the United Kingdom total fair trade sales in 1998 amounted to about £10 million, which was amazing growth from its humble beginnings.
>
> By 2007, it reached nearly £500 million.[104]
>
> By 2015, UK sales were nearly £2 billion, and worldwide sales amounted to £73 billion.[105]

And the coffee, tea, chocolate, etc., are as good as any I have ever tasted, and normally cost no more than non-fairly traded equivalents. I now buy them without thinking I am making a sacrifice. For the growth to continue, we need to keep buying more fairly traded products, and perhaps write to our supermarkets to encourage them.

Cancelling debt

In Leviticus 25:17–25, the Jews received the command that every fiftieth year should be a year of "Jubilee", when all land should be returned to its original owners. As a result, in theory, all debts were cancelled. In the run up to the year 2000, Jubilee 2000 took this principle as part of a campaign to cancel debts in developing countries, backed by a wide range of Christian and secular charities. They publicized horror stories from the 1970s of governmental aid that was really a loan being used by dictators for building palaces and buying tanks. The debt repayments then made it impossible for the countries to invest in education and health. They were trapped by chains of debt from irresponsible lending to previous corrupt governments. Jesus said that he came to set the captives free. The Christians involved in Jubilee 2000 were striving to follow his example. They showed me the fact that we can make a difference, as the following quotes show:

> For the past four years the terms of the debate have been set by the debt campaigners, who little by little have forced the plight of the world's forgotten people onto the political agenda. Not only has Jubilee 2000 been comfortably the most successful mass movement of the past 25 years, but it has also shown how the process known as globalization is nurturing its own opponents.
>
> The case of Uganda, which has had $1bn (£715m) worth of debt relief and used it to double primary school enrolment, shows what can be done. So does Bolivia, where the money is going on the poorest municipalities, and so does Mozambique, where the reduction in its annual payments from $127m a year to $52m is allowing more to be spent on hospitals and housing. Debt relief works.

That was in 2000. But as *The Guardian* said then, the problem still exists:

> But elsewhere in the world's poorest countries, children are still dying for lack of food, still falling ill for lack of basic health care, and having their futures blighted for lack of education. Despite all the pressure, despite the mobilization of political will, despite

all the promises of speedier and more generous help, that is the brutal truth. People are dying and suffering when they do not need to.[106]

Jubilee 2000 was followed by Make Poverty History, and currently the Jubilee Debt Campaign. It is amazing to look at the progress that has been made, but equally worrying to see how far there is to go.

Changing the world in Jesus' way

Fair trade and international debt relief are just two of a vast range of justice issues that we might address. More recently the Church has campaigned against the problems of debt in the UK, caused by the exorbitant interest rates of payday lenders.[107] Currently the Church of England is working with the UK government in combating modern slavery.[108] I hope that in reading the above you can sense my excitement at the possibility of us changing the world for the better. I find the mustard seed parable inspiring. To play our part in growing the kingdom of God in this way simply involves us joining in: for growing fair trade, we can buy and sell fairly traded products and lobby supermarkets to stock them; for reducing debt, we can write, campaign and pray. As Jesus turned over the tables of the moneychangers, there are also occasions for more active protests, like Martin Luther King's leadership of the bus boycott, as part of his campaign for civil rights for all.[109]

Going back to Christian discipleship, it can be costly. Jesus came to change the world by living amongst us, teaching, showing his love in practical ways, standing up to the bullies, and ultimately dying on the cross. Yet as a teenager I did not buy fairly traded coffee because it did not taste as good as my regular brand. I now do.

In today's world, some of the most significant needs are those of refugees, fleeing from war. We cannot simply give them money for food and shelter, when they have nowhere to live. What would Jesus do?[110]

Being peacemakers

Jesus said:

> Blessed are the peacemakers, for they will be called children of God.
>
> *Matthew 5:9*

I love the story of the Good Samaritan, where a Jew who has been robbed and left to die is helped by his traditional enemy, a Samaritan (Luke 10:25–37). It is an illustration that we should love everyone who is in need, and not just our family, friends and close neighbours. However, behind the story is also an extraordinary model for bringing peace, as well as caring for the needy.

Imagine for a minute that the parable was a true story. The man who was robbed was in great need. The priest and the Levite who passed by may well have thought that it was a dangerous place. If one person could be attacked, then it was not safe. The priest and the Levite had excuses. But the Samaritan risked his own safety and spent his time and money to help. To the Jews the Samaritans were the enemy. Imagine the conversation between the Jew and his friends after the incident. They would have been brought up to think the Samaritans were evil, but the Jew who had been helped could show that that was a lie. As he told his story, so healing between the nations could begin. As disciples we are called to change the world, with Jesus' methods, continuing what he began.

The Parable of the Weeds

Jesus also told the Parable of the Weeds, where an enemy sows bad seed amongst wheat. The farmer tells his workers not to pull the weeds up, because they might do more harm than good (Matthew 13:24–30). I wrote in chapter 8 of how I understand that this parable speaks of the good and bad that is growing in our world today. It is only natural to want to step in and sort out problems. But the trouble is that we can do more harm than good. I think of the frustration I have felt as a vicar, with members of my own congregations falling out. Both sides have had legitimate reasons to be aggrieved with the other. I have often come to know details that have helped me to understand why people have acted in what seems an unreasonable way, but I have not been at liberty to share those details. I have longed to bring reconciliation, but I have felt helpless. I write this because I think we need to have realistic expectations. God knows what is wrong with our world, and has chosen to change it by sending Jesus, and calling us to follow his example. We are called to continue that healing in his way.

It is natural to want to step in and rip weeds out, but most of the time Jesus' methods were different. He led by example, changing people with active love, rather than violence. As I wrote in chapter 7, his death on the cross is the ultimate model for defeating evil. For its power to be exerted today, we need to follow Jesus' example. St Stephen prayed for his murderers, that God would not hold that sin against them, and Saul was converted.[111] Gordon Wilson declared concerning the bombers who had killed his daughter: "I bear no ill will, I bear no grudge."[112] He played his part in bringing peace in Northern Ireland.

CHAPTER 16

Truth, Global Warming, Post Modernism and Politics

In the above discussions about charity, fair trade and justice I have not mentioned those who have reservations because for most people the argument is accepted, even if they don't take any action. However, when it comes to global warming or climate change opinion is more divided. As I write, Donald Trump has just withdrawn the USA from the Paris Climate Change deal. In the past he has famously denied climate change:

> The concept of global warming was created by and for the Chinese in order to make U.S. manufacturing non-competitive.[113]
>
> Snowing in Texas and Louisiana, record-setting freezing temperatures throughout the country and beyond. Global warming is an expensive hoax!
>
> Ice storm rolls from Texas to Tennessee—I'm in Los Angeles and I's freezing. Global warming is a total, and very expensive, hoax![114]

Truth is good

As I thought about whether or not to include a section on global warming, I did consider writing that we should just respond to the issue as we should respond to the needs of poverty, injustice and conflict. However, Donald Trump's tweets raised for me the issue of truth. One of the Ten Commandments is, "You shall not bear false witness". The Devil is described as the father of lies (John 8:44). Jesus states that the truth will set us free (John 8:32). When I used to watch the TV show *EastEnders*, I often wanted to scream, "Tell the truth!" The lies they told just landed the characters deeper in trouble.

To me, global warming has become a theological issue, not just because we should be concerned for our planet and all who live on it, but also because of the need for truth. It is that truth that must be the foundation for our response.

Truth, politics and popular culture

Donald Trump has not just dismissed climate change science, but he has also declared that negative stories about him are "fake news":

> The Fake News is working overtime. Just reported that, despite the tremendous success we are having with the economy & all things else, 91% of the Network News about me is negative (Fake). Why do we work so hard in working with the media when it is corrupt? Take away credentials?[115]

With worrying parallels, the campaign for the UK to leave the European Union declared:

> We send the EU £350 million a week. Let's fund the NHS instead.

But our contribution, after our rebate, is about £250 million a week, and we receive another £100 million from the EU in the form of grants etc.[116] To my mind, this slogan was a blatant lie, but it didn't seem to harm their campaign. Accusations of scaremongering were of course also thrown at those who campaigned to remain.[117]

With my logical, engineering background I find this baffling. I want to know the truth. I would not vote for someone who I knew had lied to try to get my vote. But it seems that many think that knowing the truth is impossible. Cardinal Ratzinger, before becoming Pope Benedict, warned:

> We are building a dictatorship of relativism that does not recognize anything as definitive and whose ultimate goal consists solely of one's own ego and desires.[118]

Or from 2 Timothy 4:3:

> For the time is coming when people will not put up with sound doctrine, but having itching ears, they will accumulate for themselves teachers to suit their own desires . . .

I started this book with the "Engineer's Approach" saying how important it was to listen to those who disagree with us. I believe that by looking at evidence, going back to primary sources, we can know the truth, or we can estimate uncertainty. In philosophical terms I might be described as a modernist, relying on logic and the scientific method. At Durham we were told that our culture had become "postmodern". The strength of postmodernism is that it has encouraged people to think for themselves, rather than being dictated to by the Church or any other "custodian of truth". Cynicism, not trusting everything we hear, is a strength when it leads to proper investigation. But I worry that instead of investigating, many are simply choosing what to believe or not believe based on a personal preference, or celebrity endorsement.

If this "postmodern" approach to truth means that people believe climate change is a hoax, then we are heading for disaster.

Basic facts

For any that share Donald Trump's scepticism, I am now writing as an engineer, to explain why I am 100 per cent convinced about climate change and global warming.

As with my theology I start with the facts that I consider are beyond dispute and build upwards:

- When we burn fossil fuels to drive our cars, heat our homes or make electricity, carbon dioxide is produced.

- Carbon dioxide is removed from the atmosphere by plant growth and can be stored for millions of years as coal, oil and limestone.
- Since the industrial revolution the total quantity of carbon dioxide in our atmosphere has increased from 280 parts per million to over 412 parts per million in 2019.[119] Research into air bubbles trapped in ice cores has shown that before then it had not been above 300 parts per million over the last 400,000 years.[120]
- The global average temperature in 2016 was 0.99 degrees hotter than the average temperature between 1951 and 1980.[121]
- And the fact that links the temperature and the carbon dioxide emissions: carbon dioxide is a "greenhouse gas". The more carbon dioxide we have in our atmosphere the more of the sun's energy will be trapped, like in a greenhouse. So increased greenhouse gases will result in the earth getting warmer.

The debate

All the above facts are beyond dispute. The debate over recent decades is whether these increased levels of greenhouse gases are responsible for the warming of our atmosphere, or whether their contribution might be negligible compared to other natural phenomena. Sunspots and changes in our orbit around the sun affect our climate.

To answer the question of whether the increased levels of greenhouse gases are dangerous, scientists have developed computer models of our atmosphere. They have taken into account all the known contributors to climate change. The atmosphere is so vast, and the science so complicated, that it is not possible for these models to be precise. But in spite of the complexities, they have come to a consensus that human influence is "extremely likely to have been the dominant cause of the observed warming since the mid-20th century".[122]

By "extremely likely" they mean more than 95 per cent certain. Human influence has definitely had a significant effect but given the difficulty in the computer modelling, there is a small possibility that other factors are also significant.

I wish they had said they were 100 per cent certain, but I am still 100 per cent convinced that we need to act to reduce greenhouse gases. It is again about truth:

- Firstly, the undisputable facts are like the fact of gravity on a leaf falling in autumn. We know that the leaf will fall. The wind might slow the process, but not for ever.
- Alternatively, if you had a revolver with a bullet in one of the six chambers, spun the cylinder so that you didn't know where the bullet was, and then pointed a gun at someone and pulled the trigger; then I hope you would be locked up for a long time. Using the five per cent uncertainty in the climate change modelling as an excuse to do nothing is like having nineteen bullets in twenty chambers in a gun and pulling the trigger.

Personally I am convinced by the climate change science, and the need for action. If we become carbon neutral over the next few decades, then global warming will probably level off with a rise of about 0.5 of a degree over the century, a total rise of 1.5 degrees since the industrial revolution. If we carry on increasing global emissions at our current rate, then the predicted temperature increase is between three and five degrees, which would be disastrous, especially for the poor and those unfortunate enough to live in vulnerable places.[123]

Is there no hope?

I hope that all the above convinces you, as it has convinced me, of the dangers of climate change, and equally of the need for proper investigation of the truth. I hope also that given Jesus' command to love our neighbours we would all want to do something about it. But what can we do? The opposite problem to climate change scepticism is thinking that we are doomed!

But when London suffered from awful smog in the 1950s, our country adopted the Clean Air Act in 1956, and that smog is a thing of the past.[124] In the 1970s the hole in the ozone layer was observed and the cause identified as chemicals called CFCs. The Montreal Protocol was an international agreement that began the process of banning these chemicals from aerosols and fridges. The ozone layer is repairing itself.[125] In the UK when I was a child there was very little life in many of our rivers because of industrial pollution. Again, the pollution has been reduced and the rivers are coming back to life.[126]

I do believe that global warming is not inevitable, but the challenge is immense. We can all play our part. The easy things are using low-energy light bulbs, insulating our houses and choosing more fuel-efficient cars. They will make a difference, but if that is all we do it will only slow climate change down a little.

Stopping climate change will involve us making more radical changes, using less, and making low-carbon choices in what we eat, how we shop and where we go on holiday. It will also involve decisions at government and international levels. But in May 2017 the UK set a new record producing 24.3 per cent of its electricity from solar panels, if only for a short period of time. In 2015 wind power produced 11 per cent of our electricity over the whole year.[127]

Climate change and the kingdom of God

Remembering the Parable of the Mustard Seed gives me hope. Jesus seemed insignificant compared to the vastness of the world and the breadth of history. His public ministry only lasted three years. In that time, he never travelled more than about 100 miles from where he grew up. He died with only a handful of followers, many of whom deserted him. But as the tiny seed grew into a tree, there are people in every country on earth who call themselves Christian. Like a spark starting an explosion, or a neutron starting a chain reaction, it is extraordinary the changes a small event can make—I find the horticultural analogy more hopeful than the engineering ones!

But many seeds don't sprout. Many sparks go out. How do we play our part? Jesus came to change the world primarily by leading by example. For the change to continue it involves us following his example.

In order to stop climate change, we will have to be less selfish. We need to be concerned for the poor and give up or use less of things we love. We need to love our enemies.

As Jesus turned over the tables of the moneychangers in the temple, and publicly confronted the corruption and hypocrisy of the chief priests and the Pharisees, so there is also a place for action and protest by Christians. The action will only have power if it is backed up by people leading by example.

And as Jesus made disciples and told those disciples to do the same, we need to share the truth and the hope, aiming for others to follow our examples.

Ultimately, whatever happens with climate change, I still believe that one day God will wipe away every tear, that this earth is only temporary, and that God offers us eternal life as his children. But that is not an excuse for inaction now.

CHAPTER 17

My Journey and Hope for the Church

Reading through a final draft of this book has helped me to reflect on my journey, and how it has developed as I have struggled to write. I've found my practical approach to theology useful, based on combining revelation, experience, reason and other people. I hope that the book illustrates this.

The Bible

One feature of the journey has been my developing understanding of the Bible. I am as certain as ever that the Gospels provide a reliable foundation for my faith. I am convinced that Jesus died and rose again. I can think of no other reason for the Church to start. I am convinced that the Gospels reflect the teaching of the Early Church concerning Jesus' ministry, within living memory of the events they describe. I do not believe they are without error, in minor chronological or numerical matters, but I cannot think of any reason why the Gospels would have been accepted if they did not reflect Jesus' teaching and public ministry. That presents the solid foundation for my faith, that I am prepared to trust with my life.

Jesus' death and resurrection reveal God's love, and that he longs to adopt each one of us as his children. My experience of God's Spirit brings life to those facts, enabling me to pray and discern God's presence, though in a less concrete way than the historical foundations. Those foundations and experiences have radically changed the course of my life, as they have done for countless millions of others.

Faith in action

As an engineer, I long for Christians to put their faith into action. Jesus gave us simple but challenging commands to love God, love all our neighbours, bring healing and make disciples. He showed us by his example what that involved. My journey includes highlights where Christians have done so, and disappointments where Jesus' teaching has been distorted or faith has remained as private "head knowledge". In response to God's love in action, recorded in the Gospels, we are called to help continue what Jesus began, so that others can know God's love, be adopted into his family and so that together we can bring healing and light to the world. We can be involved in growing God's kingdom.

Hope for the Church

In the last chapter I wrote of the dangers of climate change, and my hope that it could be stopped—dangers and hopes based on evidence. There are equally grave dangers for the Church. The divisions, the lack of confidence in the foundations of our faith and the lack of action have all played their part in the decline in traditional churchgoing.

But just as I believe climate change can be halted, so the decline in the Church can be reversed. My faith that God exists and loves us so much that he died for us will always give me hope. For that hope to be realized, Christian faith needs to lead to practical action.

Unanswered questions

All the above, I say with confidence. However, the journey has also involved questions to which I only have very partial answers. Why does God allow suffering? Why does he not always appear to answer my prayers? What do we do with the parts of the Old Testament that appear to betray God as a vengeful God who punishes minor transgressions with death, and who commands the Israelites to kill everyone in Jericho?

I do still believe that the Bible is "inspired by God and is useful for teaching, for reproof, for correction, and for training in righteousness" (2 Timothy 3:16). I believe that God has inspired me, yet I still get things wrong. I am on a journey. I also believe that the Bible reflects the journey that God has taken us on. The Bible contains a wonderful mixture of revelation, reason and experience, written by so many. But if we want to know what God is really like, it is Jesus in the Gospels that holds the key. As the author of the letter to the Hebrews wrote:

> God spoke to our ancestors in many and various ways by the prophets, but in these last days he has spoken to us by a Son ... He is the reflection of God's glory and the exact imprint of God's very being, and he sustains all things by his powerful word.
>
> *Hebrews 1:1-3*

Questions for a divided Church

Perhaps the most challenging question for our divided Church is: Why didn't Jesus tell the Church in advance exactly how they should behave, especially concerning slavery, the role of women and issues in sexuality? I concluded that how we treat each other when we disagree about disputable matters is more important than getting the right answer.

For this too, Jesus gave us an example to follow. Jesus prayed for those who killed him:

> Father, forgive them; for they do not know what they are doing.
>
> *Luke 23:34*

If we only love those we agree with, how are we different from members of a golf club? Or, as I am told John Wesley was known to say:

> In essentials, unity; in non-essentials, liberty; in all things, charity.

I want to build bridges not walls.

Notes

1. Christopher Hitchens, *God Is Not Great: How Religion Poisons Everything* (New York: Twelve Books, 2007), p. 150.
2. Alister McGrath, *Christian Theology: An Introduction* (Oxford: Blackwell, 1997), p. 114.
3. Thomas A. Harris, *I'm OK—You're OK* (New York: Arrow Books, 1995).
4. See for example <https://bbc.co.uk/news/uk-england-40379903>.
5. McGrath, *Christian Theology*, pp. 181–231.
6. Frank Morison, *Who Moved the Stone?: A Story of the Resurrection* (London: Faber and Faber, 1933).
7. Josh McDowell, *Evidence that Demands a Verdict: Historical Evidences for the Christian Faith* (Nashville, TN: Thomas Nelson, 1999).
8. F. F. Bruce, *The New Testament Documents* (Leicester: InterVarsity Press, 1943), p. 16.
9. James Dunn, *The Evidence for Jesus* (London: SCM Press, 1985), pp. 75–76.
10. Luke 18:35–43.
11. Mark 10:46.
12. John 19:30.
13. Luke 23:46.
14. Matthew 27:5.
15. Acts 1:18.
16. <http://www.apuritansmind.com/creeds-and-confessions/the-chicago-statement-on-biblical-inerrancy/>.
17. Peter Enns, *Five Views on Biblical Inerrancy* (Grand Rapids: Zondervan, 2013), pp. 83–84.
18. <https://www.eauk.org/about-us/basis-of-faith?utm_source=old_eauk>.
19. <https://creationtoday.org/about/what-we-believe/>.
20. John Stott, *Through the Bible Through the Year* (Oxford: Lion Hudson, 2014), p. 14.

21. F. M. Dostoyevsky, *The Brothers Karamazov*, trans. by Constance Garnett (New York: The Lowell Press, 1912), pp. 266, 269.
22. *The Guardian*, 1 February 2015.
23. C. S. Lewis, *A Grief Observed* (London: Faber & Faber, 2013), p. 58..
24. E. P. Sanders, *Jesus and Judaism* (London: SCM Press, 1985).
25. F. F. Bruce, *The New Testament Documents, Are They Reliable?* (Grand Rapids: Eerdmans, 1983).
26. Delbert Burkett, *Introduction to the New Testament and the Origins of Christianity* (Cambridge: Cambridge University Press, 2002).
27. <http://earlychristianwritings.com/text/papias.html>.
28. Bruce, *New Testament Documents*, p. 12.
29. <http://www.earlychristianwritings.com/irenaeus.html>.
30. Burkett, *Introduction to the New Testament and the Origins of Christianity*, p. 156.
31. Richard Dawkins, *The God Delusion* (London: Random House, 2006), p. 118.
32. <https://en.wikipedia.org/wiki/The_God_Delusion>.
33. <http://earlychristianwritings.com/text/papias.html>.
34. <http://www.earlychristianwritings.com/irenaeus.html>.
35. Bruce, *New Testament Documents*, p. 38.
36. Bruce, *New Testament Documents*, p. 18.
37. Burkett, *Introduction to the New Testament and the Origins of Christianity*, p. 112.
38. <http://www.earlychristianwritings.com/irenaeus.html>.
39. Burkett, *Introduction to the New Testament and the Origins of Christianity*, p. 215.
40. John 21:25.
41. <http://earlychristianwritings.com/text/thomas-fifth.html>.
42. Burkett, *Introduction to the New Testament and the Origins of Christianity*, pp. 110–11.
43. <http://earlychristianwritings.com/text/muratorian.html>.
44. Eusebius, *Ecclesiastical History*, chapter 3.
45. C. K. Barrett, *The Gospel according to St John* (London: SPCK, 1978), p. 589.
46. R. W. L. Moberly, *Old Testament Theology: Reading the Hebrew Bible as Christian Scripture* (Grand Rapids: Baker Publishing Group, 2013), p. 56.
47. Richard Dawkins, *The God Delusion* (London: Black Swan; 10th anniversary edition with new material, 2016), p. 51.

48 Jeremy Clarkson, *Born to be Riled* (London: Penguin, 2007), p. 21.
49 Moberly, R. W. L.. *Old Testament Theology: Reading the Hebrew Bible as Christian Scripture* (Kindle Location 1616). Baker Publishing Group. Kindle Edition.
50 Brueggemann, W. *Theology of the Old Testament*, Fortress Press, 1997, p. 400.
51 Walter Brueggemann, *Theology of the Old Testament* (Minneapolis: Fortress Press, 1997), p. 400.
52 William Webb, *Slaves, Women & Homosexuals: Exploring the Hermeneutics of Cultural Analysis* (Downers Grove, IL: InterVarsity Press, 2001), p. 247.
53 P. E. Bold, M. W. Brown and R. J. Allen, "Shear mode crack growth and rolling contact fatigue", *Wear* (1991), pp. 307–17.
54 John Hick (ed.), *The Myth of God Incarnate* (London: SCM Press, 1977).
55 Burkett, *Introduction to the New Testament and the Origins of Christianity*, p. 247.
56 Burkett, *Introduction to the New Testament and the Origins of Christianity*, p. 256.
57 Amy-Jill Levine et al. (eds), *The Historical Jesus in Context* (Princeton: Princeton University Press, 2006), p. 4.
58 C. S. Lewis, *Mere Christianity* (London: Fount Paperbacks, 1977), p. 52.
59 James Dunn, *Unity and Diversity in the New Testament* (London: SCM Press, 1990).
60 McGrath, *Christian Theology*, pp. 292–357.
61 <http://www.documentacatholicaomnia.eu/03d/0295-0373,_Athanasius,_Orationes_contra_Arianos_%5bSchaff%5d,_EN.pdf>.
62 McGrath, *Christian Theology*, pp. 333–34.
63 McGrath, *Christian Theology*, pp. 334–35.
64 McGrath, *Christian Theology*, p. 342.
65 Steve Chalke, *The Lost Message of Jesus* (Grand Rapids: Zondervan, 2003), p. 182.
66 John Stott, *The Cross of Christ* (Downers Grove, IL: InterVarsity Press, 1989), p. 150.
67 Jürgen Moltmann, "The Crucified God", *Theology Today* 31:1 (1974), p. 15.
68 Stott, *The Cross of Christ*, p. 109.
69 R. W. Dale, *Atonement* (London: Congregational Union, 1894), pp. 338–39.
70 Stott, *The Cross of Christ*, p. 102.
71 McGrath, *Christian Theology*, pp. 395–96.

72 C. S. Lewis, *The Lion, the Witch and the Wardrobe* (Oxford: Lion, 1980), p. 148.
73 McGrath, *Christian Theology*, p. 396.
74 Gustav Aulén, *Christus Victor* (London: SPCK, 1931).
75 McGrath, *Christian Theology*, pp. 397–99.
76 <https://en.wikipedia.org/wiki/Gordon_Wilson_(Northern_Irish_peace_campaigner)#Bombing>
77 Gordon Fee, *God's Empowering Presence* (Peabody, MA: Hendrickson Publishers, 1994), p. 854.
78 Mark Stibbe, *My Father's Tears* (London: SPCK, 2014), p. 19.
79 <https://www.aog.org.uk/what-we-believe>.
80 Bruce Milne, *The Message of John*, The Bible Speaks Today (Downers Grove, IL: InterVarsity Press, 1993), p. 232.
81 Tom Wright, *Paul for Everyone: The Prison Letters* (London: SPCK, 2002), p. 186.
82 Alan Richardson and John Bowden (eds), *A New Dictionary of Christian Theology* (London: SCM, 1983), p. 212.
83 See for example the Smalcald Articles, II.1:
Part II, Article I: The first and chief article.
1] That Jesus Christ, our God and Lord, died for our sins, and was raised again for our justification, Rom. 4:25.
2] And He alone is the Lamb of God which taketh away the sins of the world, John 1:29; and God has laid upon Him the iniquities of us all, Is. 53:6.
3] Likewise: All have sinned and are justified without merit by His grace, through the redemption that is in Christ Jesus, in His blood, Rom. 3:23f
4] . . . it is clear and certain that this faith alone justifies us as St. Paul says, Rom. 3:28: For we conclude that a man is justified by faith, without the deeds of the Law.
5] . . . For there is none other name under heaven, given among men whereby we must be saved, says Peter, Acts 4:12. And with His stripes we are healed, Is. 53:5.
See <https:// bookofconcord.org/smalcald.php#gospel>.
84 Rob Bell, *Love Wins* (London: HarperCollins, 2012), p. 4.
85 Bell, *Love Wins*, chapter 3.
86 Bell, *Love Wins*, chapter 3.

[87] Gerhard Kittel (ed.), *Theological Dictionary of the New Testament* (One Volume Condensed Edition), trans. by Geoffrey W. Bromiley (Grand Rapids, MI: William B Eerdmans Publishing Co., 1990), p. 32.

[88] Bell, *Love Wins*, pp. 99–100.

[89] G. B. Caird, *The Revelation of St John the Divine* (London: A. and C. Black, 1966), pp. 186f., 260.

[90] David L. Edwards and John Stott, *A Liberal–Evangelical Dialogue* (London: Hodder and Stoughton, 1988), pp. 313–20.

[91] Edwards and Stott, *Liberal–Evangelical Dialogue*, pp. 314–15.

[92] The West Wing, Series 2, The Midterms, Warner Home Video, DVD Release Date: 20 Oct. 2003.

[93] Richard A. Burridge, *Imitating Jesus: An Inclusive Approach to New Testament Ethics* (Grand Rapids, MI: Eerdmans, 2007), pp. 127–31.

[94] Robert Tressell, *The Ragged Trousered Philanthropists* (London: Wordsworth Classics, 2012).

[95] John Wimber, *Power Evangelism* (London: Hodder and Stoughton, 1985), p. 13.

[96] Wimber, *Power Evangelism*, pp. 44–73.

[97] Ronald Sider, *Rich Christians in an Age of Hunger* (London: Hodder and Stoughton, 1977).

[98] <https://www.theguardian.com/environment/2017/jan/10/all>.

[99] <https://www1.wfp.org/zero-hunger>.

[100] <https://www.oxfam.org.uk/what-we-do/about-us/history-of-oxfam>.

[101] <https://www.christianaid.org.uk/about-us/our-history>.

[102] <https://www.tearfund.org/About_Us/History>.

[103] <https://www.christianaid.org.uk/sites/default/files/2016-10/annual-report-15-16.pdf>.

[104] <https://www.ecoworld.org.uk/eco_topics/food/consumer-issues.asp>.

[105] <https://www.fairtrade.net/about-fairtrade/annual-reports.html>.

[106] <https://www.theguardian.com/business/2000/nov/27/debt.development>.

[107] <https://www.theguardian.com/world/2014/feb/23/church-credit-unions-parishes>.

[108] <https://www.churchofengland.org/more/media-centre/news/prime-minister-backs-church-england-drive-eradicate-modern-slavery>.

[109] <https://kinginstitute.stanford.edu/encyclopedia/montgomery-bus-boycott>.

110 <https://www.theguardian.com/world/2015/sep/06/refugees-welcome-oxfordshire-town-grapples-with-how-to-respond>.
111 Acts 7:54–60 and Acts 9:1–19.
112 <https://www.bbc.co.uk/news/uk-northern-ireland-20248737>.
113 Twitter, 11.15am, 6 November 2012.
114 <https://www.newsweek.com/what-has-trump-said-about-global-warming-quotes-climate-change-paris-agreement-618898>.
115 <https://en.wikipedia.org/wiki/Fake_news#Usage_of_the_term_by_Donald_Trump> or <https://twitter.com/realDonaldTrump/status/994179864436596736>.
116 <https://www.bbc.co.uk/news/uk-politics-41306354>.
117 <https://www.independent.co.uk/news/uk/politics/the-campaign-to-stay-in-the-eu-is-project-fear-says-boris-johnson-a6903216.html>.
118 <http://www.vatican.va/gpII/documents/homily-pro-eligendo-pontifice_20050418_en.html>.
119 <https://climate.nasa.gov/vital-signs/carbon-dioxide/>.
120 <https://climate.nasa.gov/embed/135/>.
121 <https://climate.nasa.gov/vital-signs/carbon-dioxide/>.
122 <https://www.ipcc.ch/site/assets/uploads/2018/02/AR5_SYR_FINAL_SPM.pdf>.
123 <https://www.ipcc.ch/site/assets/uploads/2018/02/AR5_SYR_FINAL_SPM.pdf>.
124 <https://en.wikipedia.org/wiki/Clean_Air_Act_1956>.
125 <https://en.wikipedia.org/wiki/Montreal_Protocol>.
126 <http://www.bbc.co.uk/earth/story/20151111-how-the-river-thames-was-brought-back-from-the-dead>.
127 <https://independent.co.uk/news/uk/home-news/britains-renewable-energy-industry-is-about-to-fall-off-a-cliff-says-new-research-a6818186>.

EU GPSR Authorized Representative:

LOGOS EUROPE, 9 rue Nicolas Poussin, 17000 La Rochelle, France

contact@logoseurope.eu

www.ingramcontent.com/pod-product-compliance
Lightning Source LLC
Chambersburg PA
CBHW070550160426
43199CB00014B/2452